Books For Believers

35 Books That Every Catholic Ought to Read

Raymond A. Schroth, S.J.

Paulist Press
New York • Mahwah

"The Stars of the Catholic Revival" first appeared in the *National Catholic Reporter*. "City on a Hill" first appeared in *Cross Currents*. Used with permission.

Library of Congress Cataloging-in-Publication Data

Schroth, Raymond A.
    Books for believers.

    1. Catholics—Books and reading.   2. Clergy—Books
and reading.   3. Bibliography—Best books.   4. Books—
Reviews.   I. Title.
Z1039.C32S36   1987   011'.7   87-13686
ISBN 0-8091-2911-6 (pbk.)

Published by Paulist Press
997 Macarthur Boulevard
Mahwah, New Jersey 07430

Printed and bound in the
United States of America

CONTENTS

CONTENTS

III JOURNALISM AS LITERATURE: THREE CLASSICS

IV AMERICAN LIVES

V THE PRIVATE LIVES OF PRIESTS

VI FORMING THE SOCIAL CONSCIENCE

VII WHAT FUTURE FOR HUMANKIND?

Dedicated to St. Peter's College, where I wrote this book while serving as the Will and Ariel Durant Professor in the Humanities, 1985–86. And to those students and fellow teachers at Fordham, Rockhurst, Holy Cross and Loyola of New Orleans who shared my love of books and became my friends.

Introduction

To Read Is To Change

To read a book is both the most private and the most public of experiences.

Private, because to do it well is to do it alone—door closed, friends out of sight, music loud enough to screen out noise but low enough to not intrude on the world we are creating within our heads.

Public in that books change us, and sometimes change the world, radically. Our social context is transformed by what we read, and, as we build our libraries the library shelves themselves take on a face—a persona—by which we present an ever-changing face and self to the world.

As Harold Brodkey writes in the *New York Times Book Review,* "In Europe, reading is known to be dangerous. Reading always leads to personal metamorphoses, sometimes irreversible, sometimes temporary, sometimes large scale, sometimes less than that. A good book leads to alteration in one's sensibility and often becomes a premise in one's beliefs."

The idea that a list of significant books is at the heart of a liberal education and essential to a lifetime plan of personal growth is an honored (and controversial) one in American life. In the 1930s Robert Hutchins, young president of the University of Chicago, attempted to reform his college, and also inspired the founding of St. John's College in Annapolis, by building the core curriculum around the so-called Great Books of the Western World; and in the 1940s Great Books discussion groups spread throughout the country.

Today, commercial publishers pour out books with titles like *Good Reading, The List of Books, The Book Book, Books That*

Changed America, and *Books That Make a Difference.* And this is one more—with a difference.

Why These Particular Books?

What do these books have in common? *First,* over the years they have sustained a special kind of popularity—word-of-mouth reputations among teachers and students, writers and scholars and general readers, as books that both delight and challenge. Part of the delight is the challenge—to stick with a sustained discussion of human values; to look with understanding into the life of a superficial, weak or alcoholic priest; to confront social sin revealed in poverty or racism; to experiment in prayer.

With this popularity requirement in mind, I have selected these titles not just by reading bibliographies, lists and criticism, but by teaching them at five colleges and listening to what students and fellow teachers say. My friend Boston College Vice President William B. Neenan, S.J. has sent incoming freshmen his twenty-seven favorite book titles for years, and five of them are included here. At the same time, these discussions have brought forth short publications like *The Fordham Personal Reading List, The Rockhurst Personal Incomplete Reading List* and *The Holy Cross One Hundred Books*—perhaps a gradually emerging canon of titles to find places in the core curricula of colleges with religious and ethical traditions.

Second, many of these books reinforce, and are in dialogue with, one another. For example, the spirituality of the *Spiritual Exercises* of St. Ignatius Loyola returns in Teilhard de Chardin, in Karl Rahner, and in every Christian's attempt to love the world without leaving it. The original, colorful news stories collected in *A Treasury of Great Reporting,* which reflect the journalists' idealism as well as limitations, set the historical contexts for books by and about Abraham Lincoln, Rebecca West and others. We must read William L. Laurence's account of the A-bombing of Nagasaki and shudder before reading Jonathan Schell's *The Fate of the Earth;* the press accounts of the Armenian atrocities be-

fore Franz Werfel's *The Forty Days of Musa Dagh;* and the 1945
stories on Belsen and Buchenwald before Elie Weisel's *Night.*

Third, most of these books deal with a group of issues that
are important to any person committed to developing his or her
intellectual and spiritual maturity through the same process.
They are: the attempt to discover the core of one's personality;
the attempt to adhere to personal values in a competitive and
materialistic atmosphere antagonistic to prayer, solitude and
self-sacrifice; the search for peace and economic and racial justice.

These are not new problems, nor is this a completely new response. Part of the inspiration for this book was Frank J. Sheed's
pamphlet, *A Ground Plan for Catholic Reading* (1938), a list of sixty
books which, Sheed explained, were neither the sixty "best"
Catholic books nor all masterpieces, but each suited to "do the
particular job" required. About half were published by Sheed and
Ward, and in 1938 their job was to do what college had most
often failed to do adequately—to exercise and "fumigate" the
mind, to instill the "certitude" that should mark the Catholic's
faith, to provide an understanding of "the great dogmas," and to
create a habit of Catholic reading—the lives of the saints, the en-
cyclicals, etc.

Today the intellectual life of the Church has changed so much,
thanks largely to Sheed and Ward, that many of 1938's authors—
like Arnold Lunn, Alfred Noyes, Abbott Marmion, Edward
Leen, and even Karl Adam—are seldom read. Only the Gospels
appear in Sheed's book and this one.

Yet, some of Sheed's principles of reading and education remain: serious reading is an educational activity in the fullest sense;
what someone reads is a surer measure of his education than any
number of degrees; the false values of the world can be con-
fronted openly by a "fortified mind"; the reader should neither
resist the writer because of the writer's ideas or personality nor
"swallow any writer whole." Sheed tells the story of the woman
who ordered her maid to throw a Hilaire Belloc book out the
window because "I won't be talked to like that in my own house
by anyone."

RAYMOND A. SCHROTH, S.J.

Why Not Certain Titles?

Inevitably, because I wanted all the books to be truly readable, that is, accessible to the average educated person without a classroom teacher, and because I wanted them to really emerge from the enthusiasms of friends, the list is not a "balanced ticket." No quotas of titles representing various academic departments, countries, centuries, ethnic groups, literary forms, races, sexes or religions.

Nor can any list or book be a substitute for a Catholic education—although anyone who reads a book like Richard Mc-Brien's *Catholicism* or Karl Rahner's *Foundations of Christian Faith* will emerge with a sophisticated understanding of a Christian's place in the world.

Nor is this a list of "Christian classics." I could not in conscience include St. Augustine's *Confessions* when I had twice given up on it, nor Milton's *Paradise Lost,* which may be indispensable to the Western literary and religious consciousness, but was aptly labeled by Samuel Johnson when he said that no man ever wished it longer.

Approaching the Books

This list departs from Sheed's in that it includes secular as well as religious titles. But is not the most important change in Catholic thought since Vatican II the breaking down of barriers between religious and secular knowledge? Although the Christian's search to "find God in all things" is as old as the faith itself, and has been the key insight of Ignatius' *Exercises* since the sixteenth century, the last twenty years have tested, experienced, and sometimes abused that insight to its fullest.

Let me anticipate the objection that in using literature for an ethical purpose we dilute the essence of literature—in that the purpose of literature is not to make us better persons but to reproduce life through art. I respond that literature has many purposes and a variety of results, depending on what the writer wishes to accomplish and what the reader brings to the text in terms of background, values, needs and openness to what either the writer or the text—even beyond the writer's intent—suggests.

In his introduction to literary study, *Passionate Attention,* Richard L. McGuire explains the four approaches the critical reader can take: (1) the "objective analysis" of the text itself; (2) the work's relationship to the author's biography or subconscious life; (3) the "pragmatic" or "affective" impact on the reader; (4) the work's relevance or importance to the various worlds to which it is related.

Thus a writer may be trying to move the reader to action, to change. If the writer does that well enough the work will, in time, achieve the status of literature and speak to the yearnings of generations, even centuries, of readers. As McGuire says, *"The reading and study of literature cannot and does not take place outside the context of human values.* Unique personal experience, from which values come, is the stuff of which literature is made."

Furthermore, is it too much to consider the process of reading, as George Steiner describes it in the London *Times Literary Supplement* (November 8, 1985), as an experience which "incarnates (the notion is grounded in the sacramental) a real presence of significant being"? Influenced by Charles Péguy's *Clio,* he envisions a "symbiosis between writer and reader." Péguy said that reading was work—so much so that only a serious illness gave the reader a chance to escape the distractions that impeded the significant reading experience. Only then could we enter the text with sympathy and affection, collaborating with its author, allowing the text to "fulfill its destiny." If Rahner can show us how Jesus can become present to us through reading Scripture, is it too much to say that serious reading can make Thomas Merton, Thoreau, and Bernanos present to us as well?

My own role is to introduce the reader to books which have affected me and which have historically affected the lives of others. Then the books speak for themselves.

I

Laying a Foundation Through Scripture and Prayer

1

Conversation With God

The New Oxford Annotated Bible with Apocrypha

In a 1984 interview in *New Catholic World,* Father John L. McKenzie, whose books *A Two Edged Sword* and the *Dictionary of the Bible* were among the most influential in teaching modern Catholics to deal confidently with the findings of modern biblical scholarship, said that the two remaining blocks to Catholic appreciation and use of the Scripture for spirituality were "in biblical and theological fundamentalism (which is really illiteracy) and a vague awareness that the Bible might recommend some changes in the Christian's attitude to the world."

The answer to the first problem is for readers to approach the Scriptures with the proper tools, aids available in the countless popular and scholarly books on how to read the Bible, and in the introductions and notes to the best new editions. The second "problem" is not a problem but the very grace which the reading should produce.

Reading the Scriptures is really a conversation between our generation of believers and the centuries of believers who have written and preserved these texts. But if a particular passage of Exodus or Revelation does not really speak to our needs we should not force it, unless perhaps the demands of a liturgical season like Advent or Holy Week make us look at some aspect of our lives—sin or indifference—we have been trying to deny.

A law student friend told me he reads a chapter of a Gospel a night. I can think of no better plan—especially since he will inevitably see Jesus in confrontation with the lawyers of Jerusalem who see Jesus as a threat.

Meanwhile, in reading the Bible systematically, it is important to remember that the Bible is not so much a book as a collection of books, the result of a series of communities, Jewish and Christian, gathering and preserving over more than a thousand years those literary works which express for all time the unique relationship which God has had and will always have with his people.

If God, by the process of inspiration, is, in a sense, the author of Scripture, he has done so without cramping, or improving, the style of the literary authors, who remain citizens and artists of their own times. Thus the drama of divine revelation unfolds in many forms—poetry, hymns, myths, history, parables, epics, proverbs, laws—recording humankind at its most degraded state and its most sublime.

The Bible looks backward in that this history of God's saving deeds should teach us something about who he is—ultimately, our Father. It looks forward in that these stories give us hope, by drawing us, through the recorded memory of the early Church, into the friendship of Jesus whose death and resurrection both point us to a future life and teach us how to live this one.

This ecumenical edition of the Oxford Bible, based on the Revised Standard Version, a more literal translation than some recent editions, is ideal for someone who wants to study the Scriptures as well as read them. Printed in a beautiful typeface, it features, along with introductions and notes to each book, several essays on how to read the Bible with understanding, modern approaches to biblical study, the geography, history and archeology of the Bible lands, and spectacular color maps of Palestine and Jerusalem. In short, it is the ideal student edition, with enough intellectual apparatus to stimulate interest in disputed questions.

What should be read? Perhaps all of it. Until then: in the Old Testament, Genesis—with the stories of creation, Noah, Abraham and Joseph; Exodus, parts of Numbers and Deuteronomy; the stories of Saul, David and Solomon in Samuel, Kings and Chronicles; Job and Psalms; the prophets Isaiah, Jeremiah, Daniel, Amos and Jonah. In the New Testament, the Gospels, Acts, Romans, 1 and 2 Corinthians, Galatians, Philippians, James and 1 John.

It also helps to recognize how these books are in dialogue with one another, that Isaiah and Psalms were the basis of Jesus' own prayer life and his gradual understanding of his messianic identity, and that John opens his Gospel with the first words of Genesis—"In the beginning"—to show us how the New Covenant has emerged from the Old.

Thus, taking our cue from John, to read the Scriptures is to understand and to participate in the creative process on three levels: (1) we see God the Creator as the source of and at work in human history, breathing life into the universe and sustaining it through centuries of interaction with mankind; (2) God enters our history, and renews creation by revealing himself in the man Jesus; (3) the Word, by engaging us in the march of history as companions of Jesus, recreates us in its invitation to a new level of life.

Let me, with the help of the notes and introductions in the Oxford Bible, select almost at random four scriptural passages which, from my experience, are rich in material for a meditative reading.

Psalm 42   "As the hart longs for flowing streams, so longs my soul for thee, O God." The author, who lives in far Northern Palestine near Mount Hermon, is prevented by his sickness from making the pilgrimage to the temple at Jerusalem. In the mentality of the time, he interprets his illness as a sign of God's disfavor and prays for healing and vindication. For us today this psalm can express the profound yearning for God which we feel as alienated members of a materialistic culture. Or the thirst of the deer for running water may resonate with our own loneliness, or remembered moments of friendship and human love which intensify our thirst for divine love.

Luke 6:6–11   Jesus enters the synagogue on the sabbath and, although he foresees that the scribes and Pharisees will use this good act against him, cures the man with the withered hand. The notes, consistent with the evangelist's intent, see this incident in the context of Jesus' attitude toward sabbath laws, and refer to seven other passages in the Old and New Testaments. But this is also an extremely dramatic story about Jesus' self-understanding and personal integrity. Few experiences are more discouraging than to have one's generous acts willfully misunderstood or maliciously misrepresented by small-minded, jealous enemies. The afflicted man does not ask Jesus for help. But Jesus sees him and feels for him. He looks around and knows that if he takes the initiative for this fellow he might make one friend (not everyone Jesus helps is personally grateful) and he will certainly make a dozen enemies by technically violating the sabbath law. Ultimately Jesus' spontaneous compassion overwhelms his human "prudence." He says: "Stretch out your hand."

Acts 5:21–42 Luke's purpose in the Acts of the Apostles is to portray the triumphant progress of the Church under the influence of the Spirit and to defend Christians against the charge that they were "destructive of Jewish institutions or a troublesome element in the empire." Again and again the authorities arrest Peter and the apostles and forbid them to preach in Jesus' name; and each time, as soon as they are released, the apostles stand up in the temple and preach again: "We must obey God rather than men."

The high priest and the council are enraged and determined to kill them. But, in a moment of courage rare among public men in Jesus' time or our own, a Pharisee in the council named Gamaliel, a teacher of the law, stands up. He argues for what we would call today the apostles' freedom of speech. Orthodoxy, he suggests, should not fear new ideas because error, in time, will destroy itself. " . . . let them alone; for if this plan or this undertaking is of men, it will fail; but if it is of God, you will not be able to overthrow them. You might even be found opposing God."

In 1644 John Milton's *Areopagitica* makes a parallel argument for the freedom of the press: "Let her (truth) and falsehood grapple; who ever knew truth put to the worse, in a free and open encounter?"

James 2:1–26 This short book, a sermon in the form of a letter, is startling in its bluntness but very explicit and practical in its directives on how we should act out the ethical teachings of the Sermon on the Mount. For example, it condemns the favoritism rich people receive within the Church itself: "We make a fuss over a man with gold rings and fine clothing" when he arrives and get him a good seat, but give a curt brush-off to a "poor man in shabby clothing." At the heart of this chapter is the insistence that external religious observance, professions of faith and pious talk are worthless without good works.

It is an early condemnation of the hypocrisy which disaffected young people saw in the 1960's and still sometimes claim they see today in a religious establishment too choked by its own wealth and formalism to address itself to the real needs of people. In a sense, the institutional Church is more devoted to social justice today than ever before; but to most Americans, including good "religious" people, the rich remain infinitely more interesting than the poor.

2

Not Beyond the Evidence

JOSEPH A. FITZMYER, S.J., *A Christological Catechism:
New Testament Answers* (1981)

A Holy Cross freshman once told me that Fitzmyer's catechism
had helped preserve his faith in the resurrection. Not because it
reinforced the popular misunderstanding that Jesus' resurrected
body was a reanimated corpse who prowled Palestine for forty
days until the ascension, but because it freed the student from that
image of the resurrection which went against his own common
sense.

A major intellectual controversy of the nineteenth and twentieth centuries which—along with Darwinism, Marxism, Freud
and the comparative study of religion—appeared to be an assault
on the truth of Catholicism was the new biblical criticism which
seemed to undermine the historicity and authority of the New
Testament as thoroughly as Darwin had rocked Genesis. Fitzmyer, who received his doctorate from Johns Hopkins University, confronts the most difficult issues, taking into account both
the pronouncements of the Vatican Biblical Commission and the
findings of his fellow scholars.

When I sat in his Scripture class at the old Woodstock College
in Maryland in the mid-1960's, Joe Fitzmyer was—along with
Avery Dulles, S.J., Daniel Aaron of Harvard and Jacksonian
scholar Robert Remini at Fordham—one of the five best teachers
I had known. To force a close reading of the text, he tested for
trivia; so you always knew you could score a few points by no-
ticing that Evodia and Syntyche show up in Philippians 4. But he

was a stimulating lecturer, methodical to the point of self-caricature, and, above all, an honest and open-minded intellectual who carefully distinguished, as this book does, between the evidence of Scripture and the later formulation of some popular doctrine.

The twenty questions raised in his catechism include: Do the Gospel stories represent an accurate factual account of the teaching and deeds of Jesus of Nazareth? How much, in fact, can we claim to know about the historical Jesus? How do contemporary New Testament interpreters understand the miracle stories? How are Jesus' words and actions at the Last Supper to be understood? Who was responsible for the death of Jesus? How are we to understand the reference to the brothers and sisters of Jesus in the New Testament? Did Jesus clearly claim to be God?

This last question, like them all, he says, depends on how we ask it. We have no way of answering it in terms of what went on in Jesus' mind, since the only documents which might directly reflect his awareness were written at least a generation after his death. The Gospels never put on the lips of Jesus the words, "I am God"; but there is evidence that Jesus conveyed an impression that he enjoyed a unique relationship to Yahweh. It took time for the unfolding of that relationship to find expression in the Johannine formula, "and the Word was God."

His most provocative question is the last: How does contemporary New Testament scholarship understand the claim that Jesus of Nazareth was the Redeemer of the world?

It could be best expressed in the epistles of Paul, who sees "the effects of the Christ event spilling over and influencing not only human beings, but even material or physical creation in general." The cosmic implications of Romans 8:19–23 "have a peculiar ring today, when we hear so much about ecology and reflect on what human beings in their greed, lack of concern for others, and profligacy have been doing to God's good earth. Environmental control is something that has been born of modern industrial and technological society, but perhaps Paul even saw the analogous need of something similar in the world in which he lived, devoid of such effects of so-called modern progress."

JOSEPH A. FITZMYER, S.J.

Since Father Fitzmyer the teacher was always slow to go beyond the evidence of Scripture, these observations mean all the more coming from so meticulous a scholar. Then I remember that one of his best lectures was on the elements of "the perfect homily": place the day's Gospel in its scriptural context; explain the terms; tell what the sacred writer intended to convey; relate it to the daily lives of today's congregation; relate it back to the Eucharistic meal. Without intending it, his scholarship is a homily as well.

3

The Gospel of Love

JOHN MARSH, *Saint John* (1968)

A first class scriptural commentary is not a mere line-by-line analysis of what everyone from the Church Fathers to the contemporary scholars at the seminary next door have said about the text at hand. It is, like the best literary criticism, a work of literature itself, with its personal style and guiding thesis. Many of the Pelican New Testament Commentaries, particularly J.B. Caird's on Luke, though briefer than I would like, and John Marsh's beautiful 704 page book on John, are good literature as well as illuminating theology.

Of the four Gospels, John's is the most prayerful: a slow, private, thoughtful reading of some of the more resonant passages—like "In the beginning was the Word," or "I am the way, and the truth, and the life," or "Greater love than this no man has, that a man lay down his life for his friends"—can itself become a deeply affective personal prayer that leads us into God's life and strengthens our power to love. For whether or not the author of John is the "beloved disciple" mentioned in the Gospel story (John Marsh suspects he is not), he is the evangelist of love, moving his readers through each sign, encounter, and long discourse into the human heart of Jesus, and through him to the Father's love which we are meant to first receive, then share.

It is also the most dramatic. Here Jesus meets secretly at night with Nicodemus, who lacks the courage to deal with him in the daylight but is "born again" when he comes forward to claim Jesus' body for burial. Here Jesus matches wits with the Samaritan woman at Jacob's well outside the town of Nablus where a stranger can still get a drink, but where the enmity between Israelis and the Arabs whose land they occupy is as fierce as that between the Jews and Samaritans of Jesus' day. Here Jesus confronts Pilate on the nature of kingship and the differences between divine and secular power. Here Jesus challenges the doubting Thomas to place his hands in his wounds.

John's gospel is also the most complex, most difficult, most highly symbolic (why six water jars at Cana?) and most influenced by Platonism, stoicism and gnosticism. But Marsh takes on these difficulties with scholarship, insight and stylistic grace.

The commentator, he says, is an expository assistant to the author, removing those cultural or linguistic hindrances that come between the author and the rest of us. Thus Nicodemus and the Samaritan woman are revealed as figures of the Old Israel searching for the Messiah, and the "doubting" Thomas as the figure of every contemporary Christian who has not "seen" Jesus but still strives to believe, and the anonymous author, called John, as "a deeply sensitive religious spirit, able to fuse together in the crucible of his own ardor for Christ the various sources, materials and ideas he gathered, and to transmit them to his world, and ours, in a way which could speak equally well to Jew or Greek, pagan and follower of John the Baptist alike."

4

Over a Beer

The Psalter of the Divine Office

"Do you have a breviary?" I was a Fordham sophomore, I think, in the early 1950's and Bill was a graduate student with whom I had been having a few beers late at night in the Decatur Bar, learning to both talk and drink, letting the world of the library overflow into the life of the pub—a phenomenon which thirty years later as a college dean I would welcome as a sign of some kind of felt intellectual life.

Somehow in those years the question about the breviary flowed naturally into a bull session between two Fordham men discovering one another and mutual enthusiasms. The group we associated with were Catholic liberals touched by what was called the Catholic Renaissance—although we didn't know the term; one of us was an early staff member of *Jubilee* magazine, another did his undergraduate thesis on the Catholic Worker Movement, and when we were seniors, one hundred and one of us published an open letter in the Catholic press attacking the notion that Catholics were or should be supportive of Senator Joseph R. McCarthy.

Of course I didn't have a breviary, so Bill gave me his, an English edition called *The Short Breviary,* and inscribed it, "Iam Foistenac Abu," which he said meant "the hand of friendship forever" and which my Gaelic scholar friend today says means literally, "Up the steady hand!" It was the most graphic demonstration I had had of the occasional alliance between beer, conversation, friendship and prayer.

THE PSALTER OF THE DIVINE OFFICE

I shall not pretend that as a priest I have been faithful to the breviary. If I recall correctly, when we were ordained in 1967 few of us ordered our own. But as my life has gone through some difficult changes in recent years and I have realized how hollow daily experience can be without reflection and prayer, I have rediscovered the psalter, specifically with the help of a compact, beautifully printed and bound little volume, *A Shorter Morning and Evening Prayer* (Collins).

The psalms work as prayers because they are both private—the solitary shepherd crying in the night—and public—the chants of thousands as they ascend the steps of Mount Zion to the temple. When I traveled abroad as a college junior I stayed for two weeks in St. Andre Monastery in Bruges where the Benedictines would fortify their community life by chanting the Divine Office; and over thirty years later, traveling alone in Yugoslavia and Istanbul, I could confront my loneliness by opening this little red book almost at random: "Defend me, O God, and plead my cause against a godless nation. From deceitful and cunning men rescue me, O God."

In *Blue Highways: A Journey Into America,* William Least Heat Moon, a Missouri college teacher who has lost his job, drives his van around the circumference of the United States trying to understand the "true" America in its small towns and less-traveled roads. Also, in search of self-understanding and his own half-Indian heritage, he brings along Whitman's *Leaves of Grass* and Neihardt's *Black Elk Speaks.* He should have also brought the psalms.

In Utah, he asks a Hopi to explain his religion. The Hopi replies: "Maybe the idea of harmony and the way a Hopi prays. A good life, a harmonious life, is a prayer. We don't just pray for ourselves; we pray for all things. We're famous for the Snake Dances, but a lot of people don't realize those ceremonies are prayers for rain and crops, prayers for life. We also pray for rain by sitting and thinking about rain. We sit and picture wet things like streams and clouds. It's sitting in pictures." So are the psalms. So is making the Spiritual Exercises of Ignatius Loyola.

5

Seeing the Place

The Spiritual Exercises of St. Ignatius (16th century)
The Family of Man (1955)

Strictly speaking, St. Ignatius Loyola's Spiritual Exercises are not
a book to be read but a manual, a framework for an experience
with grace. They are, therefore, something we do not read as
much as do.

I include them here as an invitation to the reader to make the
Exercises, in one of their many forms, because the habit of prayer
and the attitude toward life which the Exercises teach flow naturally from the meeting with God that the Scriptures provoke
and into the reading of the other books discussed in these pages.

The Exercises are a series of meditations, contemplations, dramatic images, challenges and formal prayers which Ignatius devised as he went through his own conversion, beginning with his
leg wound at the battle of Pamplona on May 20, 1521, through
his convalescence, his retreat at the Abbey of Monserrat, his studies in Paris, the founding of the Jesuit order, and his journeys to
the Holy Land and Rome. They grow from the psychological insights of a passionate man who was learning to redirect his courage, intellect and will to the service of a Savior he had come to
know in a mystical way.

Divided into four sections, or "weeks," on creation, the public
life of Jesus, the passion, and God's love, they aim to free us from
all disordered attachments which would prevent us from seeing
and acting on God's will. Finally, they try to teach us to find God
in all things, to see him living and acting and loving in every

21

thing and person—and then to return that love in service of the world.

This book does require a teacher-guide, not so much to explain the terminology as to direct the "exercitant," to help one listen to the spirit and experiment with the various methods of prayer: visualizing an episode from the Gospel, considering an item of faith in a way that moves us to talk to God, dwelling slowly on each word of a favorite psalm.

Therefore, to just read the text or sit for a weekend and listen to a preached retreat is not really to *do* the Exercises, any more than reading a weight-lifting book will put on muscles. The real director of the experience must be the Holy Spirit who will move the exercitant through various moods, images and ideas while the human director, in dialogue, helps one listen and respond in prayer.

For example, one of the remarkable features of the Exercises is a series of rules which Ignatius devised for distributing alms, thinking with the Church, decision making, and what he calls the "discernment of spirits"—which today we would call being in touch with our feelings in a way that would allow us to spot our selfish and selfless motivations. In this sense, perhaps the outstanding effect of this program is a sensitizing, a heightening of our awareness of both the wrestling match going on inside us and of the divine glory shining through every human face, oak tree, city neighborhood—and often many a printed page.

Often I find books, including picture books, extremely helpful in the Ignatian methods of prayer. When I made my second thirty-day retreat at the novitiate in Wernersville, Pa., in 1976, the house had a crumbling copy of an old (1899) four-volume (oversized) book, *The Life of Our Lord Jesus Christ,* written and illustrated by the great nineteenth century French artist, J. James Tissot, who, while not entirely free of sentimentalism, in his day was startling in his realism. Here was a Jesus with the face and garb of a semite, more like the Palestinians I encountered in the hills of Galilee in 1984 than the pale, blond, soft-voiced, doe-eyed mannikins of traditional pious art and biblical movies.

Tissot explained that he had traveled to Alexandria, Cairo, Palestine, Lebanon and Damascus in 1886, at the age of fifty, to restore to the scenes of the Gospels "as far as possible the actual aspect assumed by them when they occurred," to find the past "palpable in the actual present," to "have my emotions acted on directly by the life of our Lord, by traversing the same districts as he did, by gazing upon the same landscapes, and by hunting out the traces of civilizations which prevailed during his life-time."

I found that the hundred years since Tissot's trip have made the same kind of pilgrimage much more difficult—as I sat nursing a martini on the terrace of my hotel on the shore of the Sea of Galilee watching windsurfers and water-skiers glide across the waves on which Jesus, the Gospel says, once walked. But at certain spots, like the excavated site of Capernaum, Jesus' second home where the walls of Peter's house have been found, I was struck most forcibly by the almost scandalous particularity of Christianity—how much it was founded not just on ideas but on individuals. Jesus, whether or not he had blood brothers and sisters, had an identifiable family, one of whom became bishop of Jerusalem, some of whom may never have amounted to anything, but many of whom have real descendants whose blood flows today in the Palestinians and Jews I pass on the street.

In the first exercise of the second week, the contemplation on the incarnation, Ignatius asks that we try to place ourselves with the Trinity as they look down on the earth and behold what they behold: persons "in such great diversity in dress and in manner of acting. Some are white, some black; some at peace, and some at war; some weeping, some laughing; some well, some sick; some coming into the world, and some dying. . . . "

No book is more helpful in this kind of exercise than *The Family of Man,* truly the "greatest photographic exhibition of all time," five hundred and three pictures from sixty-eight countries, created by Edward Steichen for the Museum of Modern Art in 1955. The Exercises begin with Ignatius' First Principle and Foundation: "Man is created to praise, reverence, and serve God our Lord, and by this means to save his soul." *The Family of Man* opens with a glorious nebula and Genesis 1:3, "And God said, let there be light."

The photographs go on to portray life from birth to death— lovemaking, harvests, housebuilding, music-making, toil, famine, grief, war, and finally the famous W. Eugene Smith picture of two children, a little boy and girl (actually his own children) walking off into sunlit woods as if the whole cycle of life were to begin again.

As Carl Sandburg says in his introduction, "If the human face is 'the masterpiece of God,' it is here then in a thousand fateful registrations."

Yet the more than thirty years that have passed since this exhibition give a poignancy, and sometimes irony, to their contemporary impact. Its celebration of pregnancy and childbirth is no less valid; yet today more than a million teenagers become pregnant every year, four out of five of them unmarried. In the underclass of American ghettos, children are having children. Boys imagine that they are proving their virility, girls imagine they are filling a void in their lives, and the infants emerge into a world which can or will not care for them. We also celebrate childbirth reminded of the estimated 1,700,000 American abortions a year.

The famine pictures too we see every year—though now in color. Nor have we seen our last picture of a defiant teenager throwing a rock at a tank. Nor of the dead soldier, the back of his shirt torn open, a rifle stuck upright in the earth to mark the hole where his body sprawls, and the quote from Sophocles, "Who is the slayer, who the victim? Speak."

The Spiritual Exercises might last a weekend, thirty days, or be spread out over several months. But ideally the experience never ends. For the reader the experience comes to life again every time a passage in a book creates a presence that wasn't there before or raises a question one may have been trying to duck. And maybe we slow down and read it again.

6

Affection, Friendship, *Eros* and Charity

C.S. Lewis, *The Four Loves* (1960)

Just as the climactic revelation of the Scriptures is that God *is,* by nature and definition, love, so the final week of the Spiritual Exercises attempts to instill a constant disposition that enables one to be loving under even the most difficult circumstances.

One of the advantages of some of the best books on love and friendship—like Martin Marty's *Friendship,* Dom Aelred Watkins' *The Enemies of Love,* and C.S. Lewis' *The Four Loves*—is that by analyzing these complex relationships they de-romanticize them—silence the violins—so that love is seen not in terms of the emotions it evokes but as an inevitable extension of personal integrity, which itself can grow only out of a lifetime of major and minor self-denials.

The author of over thirty-five books, including his popular collections of radio talks, *Mere Christianity, The Screwtape Letters,* in which an experienced devil writes advice to a young devil, and series of science-fiction novels, C.S. Lewis brings to his study of love the skills and wisdom of a convert, a critic, an Oxford and Cambridge professor of medieval and Renaissance literature, a humorist, and an amateur theologian.

He begins with some distinctions: between Gift-love, by which a man plans and works for the future of a family he may die without seeing; Need-love, sometimes like a child's love of parents or a man's love for God, and sometimes a gluttonous craving for affection; and Appreciative-love, the starting point for our whole experience of beauty, which enables us to rejoice in God's glory. Then, after some discussion of what he calls "Sub-human" loves, like love of nature and patriotism, he plunges into his extended conversation on the four: Affection, Friendship, *Eros* and Charity. We can see him propped up in a big leather chair in his study, before the fireplace, waving his pipe and staring at a distant spot on the book-shelf right below the ceiling. As a result, his talk is more memorable for its flashes of insight than its overall coherence.

Under Affection—the "most instinctive," "most animal" of loves—we meet those familiar distortions: Mrs. Fidget, who "lived for her family" but imprisoned them in her possessiveness (cooking hot meals on the hottest summer days and always waiting up for those who were out late); and Dr. Quartz, the devoted teacher, who welcomed hero-worshiping students to his home, until they dared to differ with the master and assert their own views.

On *Eros,* he warns that sexual love, called Venus, is in danger of being taken too seriously; indeed, jokes about sex, in the long run, endanger Christianity far less than reverential gravity. Our sexual attitudes need less Wagner and more Mozart. Of the three views of the human body—of the pagans and Christians to whom it was the tomb of the soul; the neo-pagans, the nudists, to whom it was glorious; and St. Francis, who called it "Brother Ass"—Lewis is with St. Francis: "The fact that we have bodies is the oldest joke there is."

Friendship, says Lewis, is the side-by-side relationship, which originated in the hunting expeditions of primitive man, in which two persons discover the same truth together. Friendship has to be about some other love—of tennis, running, politics or music. Friends, says Lewis, do not look into one another's eyes. True friendship, as a love, he says, is also rare in modern experience—partly because so few experience it, and partly because some fear, foolishly, that behind every firm and serious friendship lurks homosexuality. Lewis replies: "Those who cannot conceive friendship as a substantive love but only as a disguise or elaboration of *Eros* betray the fact that they have never had a friend."

In some ways I would have liked the Friendship chapter longer, less British, less smelling of the pipe smoke of the don's den. Less masculine. He did not foresee the feminist revolution and one of its most positive effects, that men and women could more easily be friends. More about the cost, gladly paid, of life-long friendships, and what we do as Christians to maintain them. We travel across the country, or across the world, every several years to keep friendships alive. We write long letters and make and take long phone calls at night, drive hours through storms to weddings, wakes and funerals and hold hands at hospital bed-sides. We see one another through lost jobs, childbirths, broken marriages, rebellious children and loss of faith. We run, swim, ski, climb mountains, exchange books, put up with one another's quirks almost as if we were married. We drink beer with a friend for years and support him later when he discovers he's an alco-holic. Often we pray together. And sometimes we look into one another's eyes.

The final chapter on Charity challenges us to make our love, like God's love, selfless. But Lewis' best moment is his rejection of St. Augustine's suggestion in the *Confessions,* following the death of his friend Nebridius, that we should not give our hearts to anything we might lose: "There is no escape along the lines St. Augustine suggests. Nor along any other lines. There is no safe investment. To love at all is to be vulnerable. Love anything, and your heart will certainly be wrung and possibly be broken. . . . The only place outside Heaven where you can be perfectly safe from all the dangers and perturbations of love is Hell."

II

Five Long Novels
Worth Reading Slowly

7

A Harsh and Dreadful Love

FYODOR DOSTOEVSKY, *The Brothers Karamazov* (1881)

In *Classics Revisited,* a collection of short essays that appeared in the *Saturday Review* in the 1960's, Kenneth Rexroth claims that Dostoevsky is out of date, that the long conversations in *The Brothers Karamazov,* in which his characters spin out their views on moral issues, are not only tiresome but irrelevant, that the moral dilemmas of Ivan Karamazov have been "dissolved rather than solved by time." To him the book is a tragedy without a hero, a detective story without detectives, without a murderer or even a murder. And no message.

To the rest of us it is the greatest novel ever written. The one most worth rereading. As a young lawyer said to me recently, "Everything is there."

Perhaps Rexroth's debunking has the good effect of allowing the reader to approach this formidable volume with more confidence, rather than on one's knees. After all, like the novels of Dickens, who influenced Dostoevsky's style, *The Brothers Karamazov* first appeared as a serial in a journal. Written for everyone, it is first of all a thrilling narrative in which four brothers, all complicated, divided characters, struggle to solve personal problems revolving around their love affairs and their relationship with their murdered father. If it is a "philosophical" novel—as some would argue, an existentialist tract—the philosophy emerges from the conflicting personalities and worldviews of the characters, not from the author's desire to teach or preach.

To some extent, it helps to understand *The Brothers Karamazov* as influenced by the author's early life and conversion experience. Born in 1821, only a few years after Napoleon and his army had been driven from Russian soil, Dostoevsky grew up in a Russia in a state of continual upheaval, as the Revolution, which was to explode in 1917, simmered and boiled in an atmosphere of both patriotism and oppression.

His father was a poor, drunken, military doctor who tyrannized his serfs until, when Fyodor was eighteen, they butchered him. At twenty-nine he was arrested as a revolutionary, sentenced to be shot but granted a reprieve at the last moment, to be sentenced to Siberia for four years and the army for another four. In prison he met a man who had killed his father—sowing—or cultivating—the seed for the frightening idea he and Freud would later express: that every man desires his father's death.

He also came to believe during that time in the redemptive value of suffering.

His work is also the product of a stormy life, his epilepsy, his addiction to gambling, his poverty, his divided character where his conservative Christian principles warred with his capacity for evil. One contemporary wrote of him: "I cannot consider Dostoevsky either a good or a happy man. He was wicked, envious, vicious, and spent the whole of his life in emotions and irritations." Thus the human elements that tore him and tear every person in different directions—the flesh, intellect, spirit and animality—he embodies in the Karamazov brothers—Dimitri, Ivan, Alyosha and the illegitimate Smerdyakov—and God and the devil battle for their souls.

The story springs from the murder of the elder Karamazov, a cruel drunk, by one of the brothers, and develops, as we see, in the investigation and trial, the ways in which each of the brothers, contaminated by the evil strain in the family, shares in the responsibility for the crime. One is tried, another actually did the deed, but another—the most guilty—subtly disposed him to strike.

Dostoevsky has told us that the chief problem he is dealing with is one that has tormented him all his life, the question of God's existence. For if God does not exist the world is but a "vaudeville of devils" and "all things are lawful," including crime. Does Rexroth include the question of God's existence among those that have lost fascination? More likely, the question retains its force; but today, rather than conclude that moral anarchy follows from God's disappearance, one might build an ethic on humanitarian respect for one's fellow persons.

I sometimes think too much is made of the famous chapter, often excerpted out of context for classroom use, The Legend of The Grand Inquisitor. Here, Ivan, the rationalist embittered by the injustice of life, the suffering of children, asks us to imagine a debate between Christ and the agent of the Inquisition. Here Dostoevsky has Ivan express, through the monologue of the Grand Inquisitor, the most powerful arguments against Christ and Dostoevsky's own beliefs. Christ, he says, misunderstood human nature and thus cruelly asked for what man could not give. He argues that man prefers the certitude offered by institutionalized religion to the anxiety that comes with free, unconditional faith.

Some interpreters claim that the Inquisitor "wins" the debate. But the issues raised are not meant to be answered in a rationalistic debate but rather in the lives of the characters as the whole novel unfolds. A more interesting chapter, I suggest, is the later one in which Ivan receives a nocturnal visit from the Devil, a suave, accommodating, seedy, middle-aged gentleman as clever in conversation as Ivan himself.

At the heart of Dostoevsky's purpose is the saintly Russian monk, Father Zossima, mentor of the young novice Alyosha, who exemplifies and teaches the need to forgive and accept forgiveness, and the absolute demands of love. It is a "harsh and dreadful love" he teaches. "What is hell?" he asks; and answers, "The suffering of being unable to love."

At the end the brothers—those who are still alive—go on to new futures. Alyosha, who has become a hero to a group of schoolboys, gives a eulogy for a boy who has died and bids his young friends farewell, as they cry "Hurrah for Karamazov!" But now we know enough about human nature to realize how open-ended his future—and everyone's future—is. Meanwhile

FYODOR DOSTOEVSKY

Dostoevsky himself lives on in the literature that has followed him—in Andre Malraux' *Man's Fate,* in Malraux' sympathy with all his characters; in Rebecca West who uses Dostoevsky's Orthodox Manicheanism to penetrate the Slavic character; in Norman Mailer's apocalyptic world view; and in Dorothy Day, who pondered the implications of Father Zossima's "harsh and dreadful love."

8

Europe On The Brink

THOMAS MANN, *The Magic Mountain* (1927)

Thomas Mann has described this, the most popular of his books in the United States, as a "time romance," both in that it presents the "inner significance of an epoch," the pre-World War I period of European history, and in that time itself, and our perception of it, is one of the themes. The hero enters a seemingly timeless state, a Swiss Alpine sanitorium, where, free from the standard clock-time pace of the lowlands, his sensitivity to experience is so heightened that he and the other characters become representatives of the political and intellectual forces that are bringing a Europe without a value system to its greatest conflagration.

But this very long and talky book is an experiment with the reader's time as well. *New York Times* columnist Russell Baker lists it with *The Brothers Karamazov, The Golden Bowl* and *Remembrance of Things Past* as the ultimate "long read," which ate up so many of his summers that his children asked, "When we grow up, Mommy, will we have to read *The Magic Mountain* every summer like Daddy does?"

Indeed, I took it abroad and read it in Jerusalem in 1984 and Istanbul in 1985. At Holy Cross some of my student friends hated it but their professor loved it; and his warm devotion to this Mann, when we talked in the corridors, inspired me to push on through its windy philosophical dialogues to one of the most thrilling and satisfying climaxes I've read since *The Red and The Black*.

In 1912, when Mann visited his wife, who was spending six months in a Swiss mountain sanitorium to recover from a lung complaint, two specialists advised him that he too was ill—afflicted with a so-called moist spot on his lung—and should remain for the full cure. But Mann, sensing the dangers for a young person in such a luxurious use of time, withdrew, to transform his three-week visit into the story of a twenty-three year old nautical engineer, Hans Castorp, a very average—though passively appealing—young man, who journeys to the Alps for a three-week visit with his cousin and would-be soldier, Joachim Ziemssen, and ends up staying seven years.

At times, the reader, consistent with the author's 1912 instinct, almost screams for Hans to break away, rather than succumb to the aimless, seductive routine of thermometer reading, snow-watching, balcony-sitting and dinner gossip. Yet Hans pours himself into an intellectual examination of the nature of disease and the personal lives of his fellow patients and achieves an emotional and spiritual maturity which some readers describe as genius.

In one sense, not much happens in seven years. In another, since this is a notoriously symbolic novel, all the political and cultural forces of the early twentieth century clash in the personal interactions and long-walk conversations of the snow-bound retreat. The sanitorium is Europe, the world. Hans Castorp is the embodiment of spiritual Germany; Joachim, who dies because he left the mountain before he was cured to become a lieutenant, is its military ethos. Settembrini, the rationalist, liberal Freemason and Naphta, the ex-Jew Jesuit, reactionary, Christian communist, are the moral confusion of Europe. Clavdia Cauchat, the older Russian woman with whom Hans falls irrationally in love, is the emotional lúre of the East.

At the end, the "thunderbolt," the assassination of Hapsburg Archduke Ferdinand at Sarajevo, throws Hans, who has neglected newspapers, bewildered but loyal onto the battlefields which Erich Maria Remarque recreates in such gory detail in *All Quiet on the Western Front*.

In a talk on *The Magic Mountain* at Princeton, Mann said, "I shall begin with a very arrogant request that it be read not once but twice." It was not an arrogant request but an honest assessment of what the novel deserves.

9

Sensuality and Mysticism

SIGRID UNDSET, *Kristin Lavransdatter* (1920–1922)

From the testimony of those devoted to the great Nobel-Prize-winning Norwegian novelist and spokeswoman, Sigrid Undset, between the 1930's and 1950's few writers—and certainly no Catholic woman writer—have had so profound an impact on the consciousness of a whole generation of educated Catholic readers.

Many of my fellow professors and parents of today's students recall devouring the long *Kristin Lavransdatter* trilogy—*The Bridal Wreath, The Mistress of Husaby,* and *The Cross*—as one of the transforming emotional-literary experiences of their lives. And I remember Jesuit seminarians, after two years in the novitiate, where novels were outlawed and affections were usually held in check, rushing to take *Kristin* to their rooms for at least a vicarious share in her romance.

Reread today, this passionate family saga, set in Norway during the first half of the fourteenth century, sometimes seems every one of its 1,100 pages. Yet, to complete it is to both glimpse the cultural force of medieval Christianity in the farthest reaches of Western Europe, and to participate in the life, the outward ambition and inward struggle, of one of the most fully-drawn heroines of modern literature.

Kristin, daughter of the industrious landowner Lavrans Bjorgulfsson and his pious but withdrawn wife Ragnfrid, is, above all, a strong and willful young woman. Yet, along with her profound sensuality and her sensitivity to nature, there is a strain of mysticism, a longing for union with God which again and again forces her to confront her selfishness, her dishonesty, her attempts to manipulate the lives of others.

Betrothed by her father at fifteen to Simon Dare, the son of a knight, she falls in love with an older knight, Erlend Nikulausson, who is under the ban of the Church because he already had two children by another man's wife. By deception, she overcomes her father's resistance and helps to bring on and cover up the suicide of Erlend's paramour who had demanded that he marry her. Already pregnant when they marry, Kristin takes charge of Erlend's estate, Husaby, and bears him eight sons. Erlend conspires against the king, is imprisoned and loses his lands. Released by the intervention of Simon Dare, he returns to Kristin's estate. But she drives him first into infidelity, then away from his home by her guilt and self-righteousness. However, when a rumor starts that the eighth son is not his, Erlend comes back to defend her honor and dies in a fight. Kristin enters the religious life and dies nursing the victims of the Black Plague.

What is the source of the trilogy's power? Part of it comes from the rich characterization of secondary characters, like Simon Dare, who personifies what to Undset is the most important virtue, loyalty, in his lifelong devotion to Kristin and her family in spite of her attitude toward him. Part of it comes from the story itself, its sixty years of revelations of the good and evil thriving simultaneously in almost every character—above all in Kristin who throws herself headlong into life and sin until she ultimately achieves that freedom wherein God's will replaces her own. To those critics who considered historical novels "escapist," Undset would reply that the "escape" she offered is the freedom offered the soul of every human being. To her followers she was—with Graham Greene, Francois Mauriac and George Bernanos—at the center of the Christian Renaissance: an inspiring and realistic response to fascism, communism, and the twentieth century's materialistic interpretation of life.

10

The Turkish Solution

FRANZ WERFEL, *The Forty Days of Musa Dagh* (1933)

"These Turks have no pity, no compassion, no bowels," wrote the courageous young American reporter, Januarius Aloysius MacGahan, in a series of shocking letters to the London *Daily News* after he had plunged into Bulgaria in 1876 and uncovered the evidence of the Turkish atrocities in which the Turkish bashibazouks had attempted to put down a Bulgarian insurrection through terrorist methods—the wholesale slaughter of twelve thousand villagers, including women and children. MacGahan wrote, "Nothing has been said of the Turks that I do not now believe."

These reports, which helped bring on the Russo-Turkish war, contributed significantly to the public image, which has perdured into our own time, of the Turks as a race of bloodthirsty barbarians.

Yet, they were but a prelude to the story thirty-nine years later, in the second summer of World War I, of the deliberate decision of the Turkish government, the so-called modernizing and secularizing Young Turks, who had come to power in a 1909 coup, to systematically eliminate the minority Armenian population. Estimated at two million, they were skilled artisans and businessmen, deeply Christian, who had lived for centuries within what was now the diminishing Ottoman Empire.

Just as Hitler, twenty years later, as George Steiner observed, could not tolerate the existence of the Jews because their belief in God committed them to a power that transcended his own, so the young fanatical secular Moslem, thirty-two year old Enver Pasha, Turkish minister of war, whom Werfel describes as a diminutive spoiled child drunk on the narcotic of nationalism, could not bear the influence of this talented race among forty million Turks destined to play the same role in Asia which its ally Imperial Germany played in Europe.

Ironically, since the Sultans had oppressed and massacred the Armenians as early as 1885, the Armenians supported the new regime in 1908, only to find themselves victims again when Moslem mobs killed thousands of Christians in 1909. Finally, in 1915 they faced annihilation in one of the most terrible—and often forgotten—crimes of modern times, in which an estimated 1,500,000 Armenians were slaughtered and 600,000 driven into the deserts of Mesopotamia, while 300,000 found refuge in Russia.

One bold group of Armenians, five thousand from seven small towns on the Syrian coast of the Mediterranean, rather than wait for the Turkish troops who would drive them into the wilderness, took refuge on the top of the mountain, Musa Dagh (the mountain of Moses). Their fight for survival inspired Franz Werfel's thrilling historical novel, *The Forty Days of Musa Dagh*. It is the story of their young, messianic, Western-trained leader, Gabriel Bagradian, who sees himself as an instrument of destiny; a study of a community on the brink of annihilation, disintegrating physically and morally through hunger and jealousy; and a treatise on the eternal tension between those two great historical forces, Western rationalism, technology and modernism vs. the fatalism, instinct, and passion of the East. It is also a moral challenge to the so-called Christian nations of the West, many of whom—in spite of the extensive press coverage at the time—looked the other way as the Armenians perished.

"Everything on earth, not man alone, shows its reality when we make demands on it." Werfel says this of the mountain, which will shelter its fugitive Christians for a biblical forty days, like the forty days' wandering of the Jews in search of the promised land and the forty days of Jesus' fast. But he refers as well to his characters—some fictional, some historical figures—and to whole nations in the face of death or moral suicide.

Gabriel, a wealthy businessman and loyal Turkish army lieutenant during the crisis of 1908, becomes a twentieth century Moses, the sleepless military genius, who struggles to cool his boiling Armenian blood with European logic as he organizes and fortifies his camp and beats back the Turkish forces, humiliating the government in Istanbul, in one attack after another. Meanwhile, his beautiful and spoiled French wife Juliette, who had insisted on sharing his fate on the mountain, is incapable of identifying with the Armenian cause. She tries to nurse the fever victims but collapses in mind and body and drifts into adultery with a spineless Greek-American journalist. Their handsome fourteen year old son Stephan, hurt when he is not chosen as the runner to go for help, goes anyway. His corpse is returned to the camp with forty knife wounds.

In spite of the grim nature of the material, much of the power of Werfel's novel comes from its theme of Christian hope, though here Christianity appears less as a set of doctrines than a primitive, native force: the determination of most of the characters, under the religious and political leadership of the town priest, Ter Haigusun, to cling to life by sharing their resources and risking their lives for one another. It is significant that the instigator of a "suicide club," in one of the book's most bizarre chapters, is the evil dwarf Oskanian, an atheist and "intellectual," which in this context means: "a mediocre, book-learned individual, who does not feed himself by manual labor, and whose soul vacillates, since, finding no place in the raw conflict of powers, it devours itself, avid for power and acknowledgment."

Historically, the survivors on Musa Dagh were rescued at the last minute by the French navy. Readers—depending on their personal taste and literary judgment—may argue about the appropriateness of Gabriel's fate in the last chapter. To me his fate seemed as fitting as that of young Paul Baumer on the last page of that other memorable novel of World War I, Erich Maria Remarque's *All Quiet on the Western Front*.

Some readers may also fear that, like the reporter MacGahan,

Werfel is in danger of portraying racial and national stereotypes, and thus weakening the cause of universal brotherhood which the story promotes. While Werfel does emphasize the blood of his characters as a clue to their personalities, he also portrays some good Turks, like the dervishes who feel that the Young Turks have sold out their religious principles.

On a lecture tour of German cities in 1933, Werfel selected Chapter V of Book I, "Interlude of the Gods," for public readings. In this chapter, based on historical records, the saintly German, Dr. Johannes Lepsius, president of the German-Armenian Society and the German-Orient Mission, confronts Enver Pasha and pleads with him to halt the mass murders and to resolve the Armenian "problem" in a more peaceful way. "Here for the first time Enver Pasha laid bare his deepest truth. His smile had no longer any reserve in it, a cold stare had come into his eyes, his lips retreated from a strong and dangerous set of teeth. 'There can be no peace,' he said 'between human beings and plague germs.' "

As Ulrich Trumpener shows in *Germany and the Ottoman Empire 1914–1918* (1968), for the next year Lepsius, by speeches and writing, fought to raise the conscience of what he thought was a Christian Germany for the Armenian cause. But the German government replied that it was primarily interested in avoiding bad publicity for itself and that the German-Turkish alliance was too valuable to the war effort to be risked for any minority population. Indeed, the arguments for keeping the government's moral hands tied are as familiar as they are appalling: One shouldn't apply Western morality to Eastern problems; even if eliminating the Armenians deprives Turkey of the economic benefit of a skilled population they can always be replaced by the Jews!

As Werfel read his lectures, Germany was gearing up to apply the Turkish Solution to its own talented minority. They had learned from their own experience in 1915 that, for the most part, the world would look the other way as it stoked the fires of Belsen, Buchenwald and Dachau.

11

The Irish Problem

THOMAS FLANAGAN, *The Year Of The French* (1979)

To visit Belfast, as I did in 1977, to listen to combatants on both sides of the attenuated terrorism which they attempt to dignify by calling it a "civil war," to touch the barbed wire and ugly walls marking off warring sections of the city, and to be accosted at gunpoint by British soldiers in battle dress, is to weep for Ireland—and to wonder about the past and despair for the future of a people so possessed by their demons that the line seems forever lost between a rational argument and a violent quarrel.

Thomas Flanagan's remarkable historical novel, *The Year of the French,* about the now-forgotten, disastrous 1798 attempt of a French expeditionary force, in the context of the Napoleonic Wars and in conspiracy with a group called the United Irishmen, to foment an Irish rebellion to overthrow British rule, is a story about those demons. They are: the self-destructive power of the poetic imagination to distort experience by romance and hide history in myth; the wild dog of violence stoked by liquor and fueled by the animality in us all; and finally the demon of cold rationality itself, the self-serving logic of the state trained first to depersonalize its foes and then to bring them to heel.

The novel is also about history: history in the personal sense, in that each of us carries in his body and brain generations of physical traits, memories, resentments and dreams that determine every move more than we suspect; and in the academic-philosophical sense: Can we ever discover the truth about the past

43

in a way that would enable us to either overcome its impact or influence the future?

Flanagan illustrates this theme by telling his story both in fragments and several times through the journals and letters of five participants—a Protestant minister, Arthur Broome, who raises many of Flanagan's history questions; a Protestant rebel leader and his wife; a young Irish schoolmaster; and a young adjutant to Lord Cornwallis, still smarting from his defeat at Yorktown and determined to teach these rebels a lesson. Thus we witness the events of one day, its battles and troop movements, from five points of view, plus that of the omniscient narrator who wanders in and out of the minds of his principal characters—Owen McCarthy, a drunken, womanizing, schoolmaster-poet; and George Moore, a wealthy landowning Catholic who would prefer to stay above the battle and write his history of the Girondist faction in the French Revolution, but is drawn in, in an attempt to save the life of his younger brother John, at the price of his own integrity.

In one scene John, inspired by the rhetoric of Thomas Paine, explains to Ellen, whom he hopes to marry, why he must lead the rebel cause. Ellen replies that men are always taking ideas, like "Ireland," and turning them into things and places, now at the cost of human lives. Ireland, she says, is not an abstract idea for which men and women must die but what we see when we look out the window.

What Ireland *is* is a central problem of the book. To some extent, the bard McCarthy personifies the people: Catholic but still pagan; foolishly brave, yet trying to flee the battle; creative and brilliant, yet a sensuous child consuming himself in violence and drink.

My faculty colleagues ask whether *The Year of the French* will be on reading lists twenty years from now. If not, it will be because it is a little longer than necessary and some characters are flat. Nor are there any truly strong and admirable characters on either side—which may be part of Flanagan's purpose. If it is read—and I am confident it will be—it will be for two qualities. First, the power of some wonderful scenes, like the Epilogue, in which Rev. Broome travels to London and meets the mysterious "Big Lord," one of the many absentee landowners who have grown rich on the income from properties stolen from Irish peasants during Cromwell's invasion of the island. He discovers a mad religious philanthropist, devoted to the welfare of chimney sweeps and African slaves but prepared to drive more Irish farmers from their lands because their presence violates the supreme law of supply and demand.

Second, faithful to Sigrid Undset's suggestion that good historical novels should deal not with military victories but defeat, *The Year of the French* re-creates an unforgettable record of an Enlightenment genocide, of allegedly civilized mankind's readiness to sin in the name of order. The rebellion fails. The peasants do not all rise up at the French signal. The British suffer early defeats but soon encircle the rebel forces. The British send the defeated French home alive and cold-bloodedly slaughter the beaten rebels.

At the end George Moore has a conversation with a woman—who reads no history, only poetry and novels—whom he is about to marry. Her uncle, Dennis Browne, member of Parliament, remarks that he has "restored peace here." Moore replies, *"Pacem appellant."* It is a half-quote from the Roman historian Tacitus, referring to the Roman conquest of Britain, "Where they have made a desert, they call it peace"—Flanagan's final comment on mankind's folly and history's sorrow.

III

Journalism as Literature: Three Classics

12

Are Journalists Moralists?

Louis L. Snyder and Richard B. Morris,
    editors, *A Treasury of Great Reporting* (1949,
    1962)

"A good reporter," Rudyard Kipling once told Herbert Bayard
Swope, the editor of the old New York *World*, "is the noblest
work of God." Swope went on to say in his 1949 preface to *A
Treasury of Great Reporting* that "journalism is a priestly mission,"
and that newsmen should embrace and mull over this classic anthology of war, crime, tragedy and sob stories as ministers med-
itate on the Bible.

Both the priesthood and the press have changed since Swope
coined that excess; yet there is still much in the analogy that
holds. Public confidence in enough of the other institutions—like
government, the medical and legal professions and the Church—
that once emanated at least the appearance of stability and integrity has dipped, so much so that there was talk for a while that
the way might be open for journalists—aided by the unshakable
authority of cold print on a page—to make a claim for moral leadership, to give assurance that someone is taking on the Old Testament prophet's job of afflicting the comfortable and the
Christian's vocation of comforting the afflicted. But more and
more journalism just looks like a business like everything else.

I suppose it's an impression I got as a child—when I first
worked my way through the (to me) awesome, grimy city room
of the *Trenton Times* to the little gray compartment in the far corner where my father, with two fingers, for over forty years

tapped out way over 40,000 editorials for the *Trenton Times,* the *Brooklyn Eagle,* the *Philadelphia Record* and the New York *Herald Tribune.* I remember that his targets at various times were the disreputable saloons and the mayor, and that he once wrote a piece on how to drink a mint julep, and even occasional light editorials on the evils of spinach. But most of all I remember that it was very serious work and that the one quality you should have in the newspaper business (or get out) was integrity.

For the best journalists, as well as being detectives, historians, political scientists and literary artists, are moralists. That is why Walter Lippmann majored in philosophy at Harvard, and why Joseph Pulitzer insisted that his editorial writers be well read in history and law, and why people really cared how Eric Sevareid ended his Ciceronian sentences, and why Anthony Lewis for a while seemed to have taken a vow to never let anyone forget that Nixon and Kissinger bombed Hanoi at Christmas.

Thus, writing a news story or a column, deciding what aspect of an issue to emphasize—where the central truth of a conflict lies—is making a series of judgments that well from character as well as skill, from the core of the spirit, flesh and bone slumped over the typewriter, or word-processor, in the middle of the night.

I first discovered *Treasury* over thirty years ago when my Fordham mentor, Prof. Edward Anthony Walsh, pulled it off his shelf and opened it to a piece which he considered one of the best news stories ever written: Kirke L. Simpson's 1921 Associated Press report on the burial of the Unknown Soldier. It began with an allusion to Robert Louis Stevenson, "Under the wide and starry skies of his own homeland America's unknown dead from France sleeps tonight, a soldier home from the wars."

A few years ago, after I had been assigning *Treasury* to Fordham journalism students for ten years, a young man came up to me in a Bronx pub (the Decatur, then called The Lantern) and said, "You won't remember me, but the one thing I've kept from your course is *A Treasury of Great Reporting.* I gave it to my father, and he always reads it in the bathroom."

Wherever and whenever it is read, *Treasury* is filled with the "instant history," the excitement, human tragedy, blood and pathos that make journalism a profession that, in the long run, can afford to call only men and women of integrity to its ranks.

In a report that stands as an indictment of capital punishment in any age, Charles Dickens describes a public beheading in 1846: "It was an ugly, filthy, careless, sickening spectacle meaning nothing but butchery, beyond the momentary interest, to one wretched actor."

William Howard Russell, the first great war correspondent, narrates, for the London *Times,* both the Charge of the Light Brigade at Balaklava (1854) and the "miserable, causeless panic" of the Union troops at Bull Run (1861).

Irwin S. Cobb, in the New York *Evening World* (1907), opens his report of the sensational Harry K. Thaw-Stanford White murder trial with Evelyn Nesbit on the stand: "A pale, slim little woman on the witness stand this afternoon laid bare the horrors of a life such as few women have led, in her effort to save Harry Thaw from the electric chair. The woman was his wife."

But a morally disturbing story is one where the reporter is blind to his own callousness, where the reporter cannot see beyond the experience of the moment. William L. Lawrence of the *New York Times* flies in the B-29 that drops the second atomic bomb over Nagasaki. To him the bomb itself is a "thing of beauty," and its explosion, "a thousand Old Faithful geysers," a flower, "a giant mountain of jumbled rainbows." Does he "feel any pity or compassion for the poor devils about to die? Not when one thinks of Pearl Harbor and of the Death March on Bataan." In contrast, CBS radio correspondent Edward R. Murrow, in his reflections on an allied bombing raid he had accompanied over Berlin, at least acknowledges that bombing is not a pleasant job, that our strategy was a "remorseless campaign of destruction. Men die in the sky while others are roasted alive in their cellars."

Note: The editors selected Herbert Bayard Swope to write their preface and included his famous stories from the *World* on the 1912 Rosenthal-Becker murder case, stories which describe in colorful detail police lieutenant Charles Becker ordering the gangland gunning down of the gambler-squealer Herman Rosenthal at the front door of the Metropole Cafe, because, in their judgment, Swope represented what a great reporter should be. They credit Swope's role in the case as bringing on Becker's conviction and execution. "I want him croaked," the rotten cop allegedly said to his minions. And for his crime he was accompanied to the chair by accomplices with names like Dago Frank, Gyp the Blood and Lefty Louie. Alas, this reporter must record that, since *Treasury* was first published, Andy Logan's book, *Against the Evidence,* has made a convincing case that Swope was responsible for the execution of an innocent man.

13

The Doctrine of Atonement, A "Lie"

REBECCA WEST, *Black Lamb and Grey Falcon: A Journey Through Yugoslavia* (1941)

When my all-night train from Budapest into Yugoslavia pulled into Split, the largest town on the Dalmatian coast, in August 1985, I was halfway through a journey through Eastern Europe which had begun in Vienna and would end in Istanbul.

This was my first adventure in "communist" countries, an exploration of that historic corridor of the continent where Eastern and Western civilization—from the fall of Constantinople to the Moslems in 1453, through two World Wars and the Cold War—had fought, married, and fought again.

But it was also a journey in search of a woman—a writer and her book. I had discovered Rebecca West, who died at ninety in 1983, as a journalism teacher, using the rich anthology of her writings, *A Celebration,* in class. I had never met a writer who had so beguiled me by a fluent and provocative style and so stimulated me by audacious and apparently perceptive judgments.

In her biography of St. Augustine (1933) she attempted to deal with both the Calvinism in her early religious training and what she considered the irreparable harm done to Western thought by Manicheanism, as well as the tension in her relationship with her illegitimate son Anthony West, the offspring of her ten-year affair with H. G. Wells, through her analysis of Augustine's relationship with his mother Monica, whom West describes as "a smooth cliff of a woman on whom the breakers of a man's virility would dash in vain."

In her political and crime reportage, with her ability to sit quietly in a courtroom and observe the minutiae unrolling before her, and to make moral judgments based on her knowledge of history, she established herself as one of the best journalists of the post-war period.

Consider her coverage of the Nuremberg trials. The defendants, in disgrace, had lost their individuality, but her pen restored their evil individuating traits: Streicher was a "dirty old man of the sort that gives trouble in the parks," Goering was "soft," with "the head of a ventriloquist's dummy," or like the madam of a brothel seen "in the late morning in doorways along the steep streets of Marseilles."

Wounded by the fact that her father, a flamboyant journalist named Fairchild, had deserted her family when she was a child, and by her affair with the womanizer Wells, Rebecca West—a name chosen to indicate her sympathies with the rebellious heroine in Ibsen's *Rosmersholm*—made the moral issue of loyalty and betrayal the basic theme of her autobiographical novels, her post-war journalism, and her epic, *Black Lamb and Grey Falcon,* the 1181-page account of her journey through Yugoslavia in 1937.

In some ways, the country she and I saw was the same—with its handsome, high-cheek-boned, olive-skinned men, and beautiful peasant women; its string of monasteries and churches and its lively religious faith; its dazzling blue Adriatic lapping the rocky beaches, and each coastal town, a one-time independent principality, fighting off the domination of Rome, Venice or Turkey, and establishing its identity by its walls, its *corso,* and its cathedral.

But her Yugoslavia, almost fifty years before, was less than twenty years old as a nation—a contrived coalition of the kingdoms of the Serbs, Croats and Slovenes—which attempted to give equal treatment to the three religions, Orthodox, Catholic and Mussulman, but which was still torn by the refusal of each group to forsake even a part of its heritage on behalf of a new national unity.

It was also a country, exploited and mismanaged for a century by the Hapsburg Austro-Hungarian Empire, on the eve of Nazi occupation.

My Yugoslavia was a beautiful tourist attraction, with its economy in ruins, adrift in the wake of Tito's death, and as divided as ever into eight peoples, five languages, and three religions.

My Dubrovnik was a unique treasure, a thousand-year-old fortified coastal town surrounded completely by twelfth to seventeenth century walls and battlements, a city small enough for you to walk around slowly in an hour, but large enough to burst with monuments, fish restaurants, jewelry stores, and the daily lives of the families crammed into its back streets and alleys.

During the day I could ride a cable-car to the mountain top jutting up from the town gate, or descend stone steps from the door in the fortress walls to the turquoise sea for a plunge. At night there was the thirty-sixth annual Dubrovnik Music Festival, called *Libertas,* celebrating the spirit of the town which had historically maintained its independence through diplomatic skills.

Rebecca West's Dubrovnik, although she admired its exciting *corso*—that spontaneous evening parade of the populace in the *Placa*—was an historical exemplar of the moral and physical cowardice she deplored in contemporary Europe. Though a famous Catholic power, it bought its peace with the Ottoman Empire, "the devouring enemy of Christendom." While the rest of Europe fought the Turks, Dubrovnik bribed them.

Black Lamb and Grey Falcon is first a narration of her Easter-season trip, with her husband, a banker Henry Maxwell Andrews (referred to only as "my husband"), and their other companions, particularly the Jewish poet Constantine and his German wife Gerda, whom Rebecca and Henry despise and whom Rebecca uses to symbolize and typify the incipient Nazi mentality.

Second, it is a history of each locality she visits—with the high point her minute-by-minute account of the Hapsburg Archduke Franz Ferdinand's suicidal visit to Sarajevo, inviting his own assassination, in 1914. The Archduke was a great—i.e., profligate—hunter who had reportedly killed fifty-nine boars one day, 2,150 pieces of small game another day, and, in his lifetime, three thousand stags. West imagines the many thousand ghosts of his furry and feathered victims assembled at Sarajevo to watch Franz get his.

But above all *Black Lamb* is a message to Western liberals on the eve of World War II—a warning against what she considers "the lie"—the Pauline doctrine of atonement, exemplified in superstitious peasants who slaughter black lambs to please "the gods," in which the proper price of any good thing is pain. And it is a refutation of the false message in a Slavic poem about a Falcon who tells the Czar, on the eve of a battle with the Turks, that spiritual salvation follows from military defeat.

West's view of human nature, certainly influenced by her father's and H.G. Wells' betrayals, and her own two youthful suicide attempts, is a grim one. When absolute love entered our history, in the person of Jesus, she says, we killed it. Now, in the face of the Nazi menace, our desire to "sacrifice" ourselves, to work for personal salvation at the expense of the world community, was preventing us from confronting Hitler.

I know what her critics say: that she is fond of "windy generalities and hortatory moralism," that in her flashy style she inflated her ideas "beyond intellectual plausibility." I also know that I must read her books, and travel in Yugoslavia, again.

14

The End of the Sixties

Tom Wicker, *A Time To Die* (1975)

By one way of measuring, the turbulent decade of the 1960's—
best remembered for the assassinations of the Kennedys, Martin
Luther King and Malcom X; civil rights marches; and the campus
demonstrations against the Vietnam war—ended at the Rolling
Stones' rock concert in Altamont, California, when some Hell's
Angels beat a naked, fat black man to death with pool cues while
300,000 young people screamed—some in terror, most in delight
to the music.

As the rock journalist Greil Marcus wrote, the murder crys-
talized the event and the end of the decade: "A young black man
murdered in the midst of a white crowd by white thugs as white
men played their version of black music."

I would end the 1960's a few years later. On September 14,
1971, at Fordham, I walked into my first meeting with my class
on American violence. I gave out the syllabus and discussed the
books and assignments and asked for questions. A young man
raised his hand and asked, "Speaking of violence, what do you
think of what happened yesterday?"

The day before, after five days of revolt and negotiations at
Attica Prison, the New York State police had stormed the court-
yard, killing twenty-nine inmates and ten hostages. Three hostages and eighty-five inmates were wounded.

I replied that I hoped the authorities had not been anxious to
attack and so heedless of the human lives at stake because they
knew the prisoners were black. A few years later, in his review

of Tom Wicker's *A Time to Die* in the *New York Review of Books,* Gary Wills carried my suggestion much further: the white troopers, presuming the white hostages had been sexually sullied by their black captors, were more than willing to see them die as well.

New York Times columnist Wicker had been suddenly called away from a fancy Washington luncheon on September 10 to come to Attica and please serve as one of a team of observers—including William Kunstler, Herman Badillo and Bobby Seale—who, the rebelling inmates hoped, could guarantee the fairness of their negotiations with authorities. Wicker was forty-five, overweight, haunted by doubts about his own character, the values of his society, and the fear that he had written nothing that would last. He also rightly feared for his own life.

He went. The literary result is a book that will last, a morally challenging document, a laying bare of American violence and racism at its ugliest strata, and a classic of personal journalism—that difficult literary form in which the writer puts himself in the center of the action and, with the techniques of a novelist, filters the events through his own consciousness, analyzing them as they are experienced.

He gives us the autobiography of a white Southerner who thought he had overcome his own racism only to find that the issues raised by the inmates—that they are as much victims of the system as their victims were of them—had never been clearly faced.

In one of the book's most telling moments, Wicker calls New York Governor Nelson Rockefeller to plead with him to hold off the attack, to come to Attica and talk *with the observers,* to "gain time" by demonstrating that he cared about the inmates and the hostages, "to understand the threat of bloodshed in its full dimension."

Rockefeller replied that the issue was amnesty and that granting amnesty would violate equal application of the laws. Wicker wanted to laugh: many of the inmates were there because of *un*-equal application of the laws. To Wicker, the power establishment had lost a sense of the value of human life. ". . . to the

Rockefellers of the world, those institutions, processes, and arrangements by which humans had sought to order their affairs had become, finally, more important than the people who had erected them and sought to live by them."

When the smoke cleared and the bodies were counted, Wicker returned home overcome by failure. He had learned more things than he had wanted to know. But he had also learned to look at a murderer, rapist and thief and say that this too is a human being.

IV
American Lives

15

The Lonely Man

Henry David Thoreau, *Walden* (1854)

Martin E. Marty takes the title of his history of American religion, *Pilgrims in Their Own Land,* from Jacques Maritain's *Reflections on America:* "Americans seem to be in their own land as pilgrims, prodded by the dream. They are always on the move—available for new tasks, prepared for the possible loss of what they have. They are not settled, installed. . . ." In fact, says Maritain, some aspects of this American mood are close to "Christian detachment, to the Christian sense of the impermanence of earthly things."

I fear that a contemporary observer of the American scene would be slow to find evidence of "Christian detachment." But it does appear from time to time in the lives of those we choose to respect—even if we cannot emulate.

Thoreau would not call his detachment Christian. As Marty says, in leaving the Unitarian church he turned nature into a church, and he became a forerunner of the millions who claimed to hear not only a different drummer but even a personal drummer, who turns soul-searching into an entirely private affair.

But, paradoxically, few private persons have had so broad and long an impact. Known for his knowledge of little Concord, few men of his time traveled more widely—exploring Maine, Cape Cod and Minnesota—and no one recorded more faithfully, nor more beautifully, the details of what he saw: the flying squirrel, the playful diving loon, the mist on the surface of the lake, the woodchuck stealing across his path, the sound of raindrops on cedar splints which covered his roof.

However, in seventeen years of teaching *Walden* I have found that the first student reaction to Thoreau is to resist him, to look for inconsistencies in his behavior, to latch onto evidence that will undermine the moral authority of his message—for example, that the inspiration to write "Civil Disobedience" was the result of one night in jail, or that rather than live like a real hermit at the pond, he daily sauntered into town where he got a free lunch from his aunt.

Students initially resist Thoreau because, at first glance, he seems to be all the things American adolescents don't want to be—unpopular, alone, left out, resented to this day by the descendants of the townspeople who 140 years ago saw him as a strange young fellow who had no steady job and who accidentally or deliberately set one of their fields on fire.

Some of their resistance is prudent. We swallow no author whole. Thoreau did not have everything we look for today in the mature, well-integrated person. The critic Carl Bode, in an examination of Thoreau's unconscious, mentions that his personal relationships were thwarted by Thoreau's inability to outgrow his mother fixation, that he could not talk to younger women, that he compensated for his inability to establish normal friendships by excessive aggressiveness and independence. His resistance to the authority of his parents made him resent the authority of the state.

But the miracle of Thoreau—as with most great artists—is that the truth and power of his writing transcended the limitations of his personality. And few lives, short as his was, had more singleness of purpose.

Thoreau's "steady job" was indistinguishable from his life. Though semi-skilled as a teacher, naturalist, surveyor, pencil-maker and lecturer, he was above all a writer—subordinating all other activities, a job, a social life, friendships—to his journal, the raw material of his essays and books, above all *Walden,* which may well be the greatest American book.

So it is both ironic and sad that this relatively young man with

a fundamental message for the world reached so few readers before his death of tuberculosis at forty-four. Seven hundred and
six (out of a printing of one thousand) unsold copies of *A Week
on the Concord and Merrimac Rivers* (1849) cluttered the attic of his
parents' home, and *Walden* (1854), distilled from his journals after
two years (1845–1847) in a ten-foot by fifteen-foot cabin he built
himself in a cove on Walden Pond, was barely noticed.

But even if students are put off by Thoreau at first, if they give
him a chance, if they walk with him through the pine forest, ad-
mire the gentle rain that waters his bean patch, listen to the Concord church bells reverberating through the fog, sense his kinship
with the badger and the loon, and, on a warm or chilly day
plunge into the pond for a swim, they are drawn toward him in
a lifelong relationship—because he deals with the fundamental
human need: to discover, through reflection on immediate experience, what it means to be an individual person, "to live deep
and suck out all the marrow of life."

Walden deals, as Perry Miller says, with some "Eden of the
soul in which at least one American held off the pressure of ma-
teriality and mediocrity."

Contrary to myth, Thoreau did not live as a recluse but, to
hear some of the gossip, sauntered almost daily into Concord,
frequently lunching with his aunt, and occasionally entertained
crowds of picnickers—plus a steady stream of curiosity seekers
who pretended to be asking for a glass of water. He pointed to
the pond.

In the morning he plowed his bean field, read and wrote—and
took a swim. On his walks and boat rides he observed and engaged muskrats, fish and loons as consciously and personally as
he did his fellow men and women—sometimes more so. In the
croaking of Walden's frogs he hears the croaking of every frog in
America communicating with one another; and in the Sunday
churchbells he hears the vibratory hum of pine needles as if they
had become the strings of a harp.

Unified around the seasons of one year, *Walden* takes on the
rhythm of nature's own death and rebirth as, in the climactic
chapter, spring cracks the pond's ice, and Thoreau decides: "I left

the woods for as good a reason as I went there. Perhaps it seems to me that I had several more lives to live, and could not spare any more time for that one."

He had heard the "different drummer" again and was stepping out to be himself somewhere else.

E.B. White, in his delightful 1939 essay, "Walden," writes Henry a letter after his own visit to the pond where, he reports, the full, clear croak of the frog, hoarse and solemn, still bridges the years, but there are two beer bottles in the ruins of the old hut.

I have been there three times in the last ten years, twice with students, in the summer and in the fall, to walk along the edge of the water through the pines to Henry's cove for a swim.

One time I walked into Concord, past Emerson's home, to Sleepy Hollow Cemetery and sat quietly by Henry's grave and contemplated the cricket perched confidently on his little stone.

16

Manhood

STEPHEN B. OATES, *With Malice Toward None: The Life of Abraham Lincoln* (1977)

In his preface, Stephen B. Oates, who is also the biographer of Nat Turner, John Brown and Martin Luther King, explains that he has not sought to "canonize or denigrate" Lincoln, "but to draw a portrait that is fair and unflinching in its realism . . . to give him something to which he is entitled: his right to be a human being."

All the more fitting then that the human being who emerges from the majestic agony of this story is a saintly man—a man who stands broken and in pain before Providence, yet strong before the nation that leans on him for strength.

Young Lincoln's favorite book was Parson Weems' *Life of Washington;* at nineteen, inspired by the excitement of hanging around the log court houses, he read the *Revised Statutes of Indiana,* the Declaration of Independence and the Constitution.

When he ran for the legislature at twenty-three he said: "I have no other [ambition] so great as that of being truly esteemed of my fellow men, by rendering myself worthy of their esteem."

All his life Lincoln struggled with a deep depression brought on by extreme anxiety, overwork and exhaustion, and aggravated by a seemingly endless succession of handicaps and tragedies—the poverty and illiteracy of his parents; rejections by Mary Todd's family; the deaths of his sons Eddie at four, and Willie, in the White House, at eleven; the progressive madness of his wife; the petty betrayals of politicians; the collective suffering of the shattered nation which, as he saw it in his dreams, had become a phantom vessel, with himself at the helm, moving swiftly toward a distant shore, where God's mysterious will would prevail, but only after the sin of slavery had been purged.

Above all, Lincoln refused to be small, to bargain away essential principles to pacify opponents who, he knew, ultimately wanted not reasonable accommodation but moral surrender.

In his first Inaugural Address he predicted that some day "the better angels of our nature" would touch the mystic chords of memory to "swell the chorus of the Union."

Until that time, his personal courage would hold the American spirit together. When the siege of Fort Sumter had begun, some Maryland leaders came to implore that he make peace with the South "on any terms." Lincoln replied, "The rebels attack Fort Sumter, and your citizens attack troops sent to the defense of the government, and the lives and property in Washington, and yet you would have me break my oath and surrender the Government without a blow. There is no Washington in that—no Jackson in that—no manhood nor honor in that."

17

The Catholic Revolutionary

DOROTHY DAY, *The Long Loneliness* (1952)

Of the three greatest American women—Jane Addams, Eleanor Roosevelt and Dorothy Day—I dare to suggest that, in spite of Mrs. Roosevelt's pre-eminence, the influence of Dorothy Day may eventually be the longest and most deeply felt.

Jane Addams and Dorothy Day gained national prominence by establishing an institution—Hull House in Chicago/the Catholic Worker in the Bowery—to meet the needs of the inner-city poor; and both lost national acceptance when they followed through on the international implications of their values—from fighting poverty to embracing pacifism.

Theodore Roosevelt called Addams a "Bull Mouse"; during World War I she was denounced as a radical, a Bolshevist, "the most dangerous woman in America." Because of its pacifism, the nationwide Catholic Worker movement shrunk to a few Houses of Hospitality during World War II—only to take on new life in the 1960's as the movement's non-violent philosophy provided the moral underpinnings for opposition to the war in Vietnam. Once in 1936, when Dorothy saw 108 homeless Arkansas farmers living in tents by the roadside, her first response was to telegraph Mrs. Roosevelt to do something about it. Mrs. Roosevelt responded through the bureaucracy; but she did so immediately. Somehow Dorothy Day had sensed a kindred spirit and had not been wrong. Meanwhile, anyone who admired Mrs. Roosevelt in her lifetime will remember how much she, like Addams and Day, was vilified as a radical, although her views were much more conventional than those of the other two. It is hard to avoid the conclusion that all three were reviled as busy-bodies and do-gooders because they were strong, independent, fearless women wielding political and moral influence in a world usually run exclusively by men.

Dorothy Day's influence will endure because she was, with the French agrarian visionary Peter Maurin, the founder of a movement that combined Christian philosophy, agrarianism, socialism, pacifism, anarchism, journalism and strong personalities to create almost a half-century of leftist intellectual life in the American church, all the while with scrupulous obedience to ecclesiastical authorities.

Her spiritual family includes Michael Harrington, author of *The Other America;* the Association of Catholic Trade Unionists; Thomas Merton; Daniel Berrigan, S.J.; John Cogley, an editor of *Commonweal* and at the *New York Times;* generations of readers of the *Catholic Worker;* Cesar Chavez; James Douglas, who helped draft the Vatican Council's statement on peace; countless draft resisters; and thousands of nameless poor who have filed through her Bowery soup kitchen for a meal and a bed.

Her autobiography, *The Long Loneliness,* is by no means the whole story of her life, which she has told in several memoirs and an autobiographical novel. It is a "confession." She says: "Going to confession is hard. Writing a book is hard, because you are 'giving yourself away.' But if you love, you want to give yourself." She begins with her Brooklyn childhood and ends with Peter Maurin's death; in between she recounts her pilgrimage—as a journalist, a Greenwich Village bohemian, a political agitator, world traveler, and convert. She passes over an abortion and a brief first marriage, but dwells lovingly on her common law marriage with Forster Batterham, whose child, Tamar, she bore but whom she left so she and her daughter could become Catholics.

Rereading *The Long Loneliness,* along with a 1968 collection of articles from the *Catholic Worker* edited by Thomas C. Cornell and James H. Forest, *A Penny a Copy,* suggests that the word which best describes Dorothy Day is revolutionary. Revolution is fundamentally the reorientation and realignment of a whole system of values; Dorothy Day's contribution to such a shift of values makes her one who bridges the gap between generations and a symbolic mother of much of the American church.

Through her indiscriminate and uncompromising love of the Mystical Body in all its attractive and unattractive parts—Eugene O'Neill reciting "The Hound of Heaven" to her in a Fourth Street saloon back room; Max Bodenhein taking refuge in drink because drink was easier to get than bread; Elizabeth Gurley Flynn, the communist whom Dorothy saw as fulfilling the first law of Christ—she has given the word "catholic" its fullest extension, and she has vastly expanded our understanding of the concept of violence.

For her, violence is President Truman "jubilant" over the deaths of 318,000 Japanese. "It is to be hoped they are vaporized," she wrote caustically in the September 1945 *Worker,* "our Japanese brothers, scattered, men, women and babies, to the four winds, over the seven seas. Perhaps we will breathe their dust into our nostrils, feel them in the fog of New York on our faces, feel them in the rain on the hills of Easton." Violence is the lay trustees of St. Patrick's Cathedral, who broke the graveyard strike in 1949, who "could not treat with Catholic workingmen as human beings and brothers."

Before she died in 1980, although I knew several of her friends through *Commonweal,* I saw her only a few times and met her only once. A few years before her death she came to a memorial Mass at St. Joseph's Church in the Village for John Cogley, the most admired Catholic writer of his time, whose intellectual integrity and desire to be an Anglican married priest led him to leave the Church. I concelebrated the Mass and gave her Communion. In *The Long Loneliness* she describes herself kneeling in that same church in her youth attending early Mass after a night in the taverns—not knowing what was going on at the altar but comforted by the lights and silence.

Perhaps it seems foolish to take comfort in the survival of her reputation at a time when there is so much evidence that her revolution has failed. Yet no one knew better than she how the progress of a revolution is measured in a series of failures—how every freezing picket line, every blow suffered, every night endured in jail, both participates in the apparent failure of the cross and, at the same time, moves a whole culture farther away from those attitudes which, in an acquisitive and property-centered society, are more violent and toward those which are more non-violent: from the ruggedly individualistic toward the collective; from the competitive toward the cooperative; from the economic toward the humane. Dorothy Day entered each battle willing, half expecting, to lose.

18

The Angel at the Door

THOMAS MERTON, *The Seven Storey Mountain* (1948)

Early in his *Blue Highways* journey through America's back roads in search of America and himself, William Least Heat Moon pulls his van into a Cistercian monastery in Georgia. Though a non-believer, he joins the monks at meals and prayer and engages two in long personal conversations about their vocations. As he browses in the abbey bookstore and picks up a volume that catches his attention, a monk virtually commands, "That's the one to read."

Believers and others have been saying that about *The Seven Storey Mountain* for almost forty years. The author of fifty books and the subject of over twenty, no pilgrim—in Marty's and Maritain's sense of that word—has caught hold of the modern American religious imagination like Thomas Merton.

Like Thoreau, in his solitude he seems to personify so much of what Americans fear; yet in his asceticism, his hard-won peace of soul, he also represents what Americans most need.

When I was in the Army artillery at Fort Bliss, Texas, in 1955, where our Saturday night pleasure was taking in the night life of Juarez, Mexico—considered one of the great "sin cities" of the world—one of our Fordham crowd in the BOQ loved to suddenly read out loud to us from Merton's *Seeds of Contemplation*. If the readings seemed incongruous to any of us in the wake of our carousings, that was only because we had not yet read the autobiography of that complex, brilliant, restless young man whose thirst for knowledge—then for understanding—led him into Catholicism, and into a Trappist monastery.

I reread it, half expecting to find a period piece, a nostalgic reminder of what was most attractive about Catholicism—the mysteriousness of the ritual, the order of its intellectual system—at a time when post-World War II America was grasping for a symbol of stability, before the 1960's swept the order away. I found instead one of the great American autobiographies—like the stories of Jane Addams, Dorothy Day and Malcolm X—a conversion story, mingling witness and confession, testimony that our lives do not tumble along haphazardly but develop, often to our surprise, according to some inscrutable plan.

Readers of the recent biographies, and of the very interesting book of recollections edited by Paul Wilkes, *Merton, By Those Who Knew Him Best,* know that he was—and became—a much more complex, even contradictory, individual than the young convert who, in *The Seven Storey Mountain,* warned his readers a bit too often that hell was not so far away. The obscurity that seemed his choice when he entered Gethsemani as World War II broke out did not characterize his career. In his writings on race and war he became an international force; and the young man led to Catholicism by the very European writings of Blake, Gilson, Maritain and Hopkins became a spiritual bridge to the East—until his bizarre death by accidental electrocution at an ecumenical Buddhist conference in Bangkok at only fifty-three in 1968.

Like Dorothy Day, he passed over, or merely hinted at, some of the rougher periods of his pre-conversion life, like his love affairs and his illegitimate child who died during the war. And the readers of his spiritual books who might have heard that he had withdrawn from the big monastery residence to a Walden-like hut in the woods knew little of his friends who would meet him outside the hermitage with a six-pack or of his attachment for a young woman who, a few years before his death, he just had to see.

Yet none of this detracts from the fascination with his ascent up the metaphorical seven steps of Dante's *Purgatorio* to peace, as he saw it in 1948. The most powerful passages include his description of Columbia professor Mark Van Doren as the great teacher who came to class loaded with real questions he cared about; his experience working with the interracial Friendship House in Harlem—the neighborhood he saw as a "living condemnation of our so-called 'culture' . . . a divine indictment against New York City and the people who live downtown and make their money downtown"; and his carefully worked-out moral decision to join the army as a non-combatant—until he flunked the physical for not having enough teeth.

After thirty years, the one episode I remembered from my first reading was the scene where a mysterious stranger comes to young Merton's New York apartment explaining that he knew someone who had read his recent review in the *Times* and that therefore Merton might give him money to get home to Connecticut! Merton had just been making the Spiritual Exercises of St. Ignatius—not with a guide, but reading them on his own—and had been meditating, legs curled up Zen fashion, on the rules for giving alms when he heard the knock at the door. His visitor, he concluded, might well be an angel. You never know when God is going to knock and give you a chance to practice what you're praying about.

19

Not Afraid To Change

The Autobiography of Malcolm X (1964)

To the central theme of American black literature—what it means to be a black American, and to struggle to express that black self-consciousness in a dominantly white, urban culture with a history of oppressing the black race—*The Autobiography of Malcolm X* brings the added dimension of another theme prominent in American autobiography, the conversion experience.

In *Native Son,* Richard Wright shocked America in the portrait of Bigger Thomas, the young Chicago black man who accidently kills a young white woman in a moment of passion and fear, and who murders his own girl friend, is trapped and tried and goes to death affirming his crime, refusing the consolations of either religion or ideology.

His was a rage articulated more softly in Ralph Ellison's *Invisible Man* in the 1950's, then with renewed heat in James Baldwin's essays and novels in the 1960's. Both Ellison and Baldwin were Wright's literary sons; but Malcolm X captured Wright's spirit in a more dramatic way: in some ways, although he was not a murderer, he personified in his own life and public image what Bigger Thomas represented: the black man as threat—he frightened whites, excoriated them with his eloquence and wit, and his followers loved him for it.

At the same time, Malcolm X's story is in the tradition of *The Education of Henry Adams,* in its attempt to catch a life pulled along by historical forces in a world of fast-paced change, and of Jane Addams' *Twenty Years at Hull House* in its attempt to explain to

76

an admiring public what brought this individual to this point in life and made him or her somehow a model for all Americans. For Jane Addams it was the childhood influence of Abraham Lincoln and the quasi-mystical insight at a bullfight in Spain that she was wasting a life that should be spent in the service of others. For Malcolm X it was the discovery of Allah.

On a walk through Harlem not long ago I stopped in the Liberation Book Store to find displayed an old poster of Malcolm standing by a window brandishing a sub-machine gun, over a quote from one of his speeches, "By Any Means Necessary." The actual scene may well have represented not Malcolm's leading an armed struggle against white society but protecting himself from the black assassins who gunned him down in the Audubon Ballroom, February 21, 1965. We remember the photographs of him dead, with thirteen bullet holes in his chest, and we also remember that many good white people felt relieved that he was gone.

A "violent" and "irresponsible" threat to gradual racial harmony had been removed. And was there not, apparently, an explanation for his fate? The monster Hate had revisited its maker and given him his due. Shortly before his death, Malcolm X had predicted he would be killed and that the white man, in his press, would identify him with "hate." Yet today, a slow reading of *The Autobiography of Malcolm X* reveals not a hater but a pilgrim.

With its pattern of fall, grace, redemption and death, the *Autobiography* can be read as a religious testimony consistent with Karl Rahner's thesis that anyone who courageously accepts life has already accepted God, "for anyone who really accepts *himself,* accepts a mystery in the sense of the infinite emptiness which is man."

At the same time, the book is an indictment of American private morality. Speaking mainly of the so-called respectable upper-classes he writes: "As I got deeper into my own life of evil, I saw the white man's morals with my own eyes. I even made my living helping to guide him to the sick things he wanted." Nevertheless, Malcolm was an extremely intelligent young man looking for meaning in his life and discovering his deepest self in the

77

very quality that had made him an object of hatred—his black-ness.

Malcolm tells his story, through black journalist Alex Haley, author of *Roots,* with some anger, but with no self-pity. When he was in the eighth grade he had wanted to be a lawyer. A teacher set him straight: he was a nigger and should stick to his carpenter's bench. His father, a Baptist minister and organizer for the Universal Negro Improvement Association, had his head crushed and his body tossed under a street car in Omaha. His mother lost her mind under the strain of caring for the family. In Malcolm's memory, this was society penalizing its members who could not stand up under its weight. "Big Red," as he was called, became a pimp and an armed robber and was sentenced to prison.

He read constantly: the dictionary, encyclopedias, Will Durant, Gregor Mendel, Spinoza, Shakespeare. He became convinced that the black people had a glorious history that white historians had suppressed. He heard of Chicago's Elijah Muhammed, Messenger of Allah, the Shepherd of the Nation of Islam in the Wilderness of the United States, and adopted the rigorous Muslim moral code.

He learned to pray. "I had to force myself to bend my knees. And waves of shame and embarrassment would force me to back up. For evil to bend its knees, admitting its guilt, to implore the forgiveness of God, is the hardest thing in the world." He turned to Elijah Muhammed—very much as James Baldwin had in *The Fire Next Time*—in search of a father, in search of his own name. But, unlike Baldwin, who rejected Muhammed for his simple dogmatism, Malcolm X became his prophet.

After his release, Malcolm became Elijah's most successful organizer, but his very success seemed to jeopardize Elijah's authority. In March 1964, disillusioned by Muslim aloofness from the civil rights struggle and what he learned about Elijah's personal life, Malcolm broke away. At this time of personal upheaval, he made a pilgrimage to Mecca, where he was shaken by the further realization that the "white devils" he had learned to hate could also be his brothers. The new Malcolm, aware of a plot to kill him, continued to travel in Africa and the Middle East, internationalizing the American racial issue, planning to bring it before the United Nations, rethinking his previous convictions, groping for a new identity in the new society he wanted to help create.

The Liberation Book Store also displayed an announcement of a rally to celebrate Malcolm's memory. The *Autobiography* is slowly being accepted as a "classic," but America is still far from comprehending the significance of this too brief life. No eternal flame burns on his grave; few white men see any significance in his life or feel their lives diminished by his passing. Yet, in a quick, tragic existence he achieved in heroic manner what society usually credits to sages and saints: he had changed.

He had come to know, without flinching, the evil in himself and the world. He had opened his soul enough to cleanse it and glimpse the previously invisible bonds that linked him to men and women of all classes and colors.

Expecting to die any minute, he clung to life so that something could be achieved by his perseverance in his last days. "I know," he wrote, "that societies often have killed the people who have helped to change those societies. And if I can die having brought any light, having exposed any meaningful truths that will help to destroy the racist cancer that is malignant in the body of America—then, all of the credit is due to Allah. Only the mistakes have been mine."

20

The Stars of the Catholic Revival

WILFRID SHEED, *Frank and Maisie: A Memoir With Parents* (1985)

Like all those physical and personal traits of our parents that lie dormant in our bodies waiting to break through in middle age, this autobiographical recollection of the writers and publishers Frank Sheed and Maisie Ward has been in Wilfrid Sheed's genes.

Much of his work—his essays and eight novels—has crossed back and forth between confession and reticence. His reviews, as he says in *The Good Word,* tend to cross reference literature with life. With his Catholic sensibility he is fine-tuned to understand the central theme of Mary Gordon's *Final Payments,* the obligation to love the unlovable; and when he reviews Norman Mailer's *Miami and the Siege of Chicago,* he writes as a one-time brother "peacenik" who had marched to the 1968 Democratic Convention with Gene McCarthy only to see the "war party" mount in his place "a China doll with the voice of a manic spinster." Meanwhile, his novels spring from his life as a student and as a critic; and in his criticism, in the best tradition of the essay, he ends up talking about himself—but without indulging the "I" and without telling us more than we want to know, and often telling us less.

Furthermore, the Sheed-Ward family for generations has written books about itself without telling its secrets. Maisie's father Wilfrid wrote a biography of Newman and one of his own father William. Maisie wrote a biography of her father, another of Newman, and her own autobiography, *Unfinished Business* (1964), where she anticipates the wit of her son in her observation that the Modernist crisis might never have developed the way it did if one of its hero-victims, Father Tyrrell, had only had a stronger chin, and thus not been so susceptible to the ideas of others. And Frank wrote his own story in *The Church and I* (1974), where, reflecting on his fifty years as a street-corner lay preacher, he tells us that "the principal fact of life" in religious argument "is that one must never talk for victory" because sooner or later you will cheat.

Frank and Maisie: A Memoir with Parents is part autobiographical essay, part intellectual history of the American Catholic Church after World War II, part religious testimony—almost as if Wilfrid, in spite of his personal wounds, shyness, and sometimes ambiguous status as a "Catholic" writer, has stepped onto the lecture platform from which his beloved parents, worn out, had fallen.

The son has not organized his testimony well. He has barely organized it at all. Rather, he has spun together collections of recollections around general headings: moves back and forth between America and England; his own adolescent polio attack; the role of Sheed and Ward as publishers in laying the intellectual groundwork for Vatican II; the bitter-sweet aftermath in which the rock of the literal interpretation of the Gospels on which Frank had built his vision of the Church seemed to turn to sand, and their son and daughter saw their marriages wash away. Through it all the Sheeds carry on like a cross between a band of itinerant missionaries and a vaudeville team, singing, dancing, and whistling their way through the twentieth century Church and world.

Perhaps because he lived longer and must still be a powerful presence in the author's psyche, Frank tends to dominate the story. As a young man, he escaped a brilliant but brutal and drunken Marxist father in Sydney, Australia, to move to London and marry Maisie Ward, eight years his senior, member of an English family so Catholic and so well-connected that Cardinal

Newman seemed a constant presence in the house years after he died and G.K. Chesterton would stop by to bounce Wilfrid, his godson, on his knee.

Soon, Frank's mother Minny followed him and became, in a way, Wilfrid's second mother when, in 1940, the clan fled the war to America and Sheed and Ward, publishers and lecturers, toured the English-speaking world building an audience for their books and corralling mystics, theologians and reformers who had their own books perking away inside.

Thus Sheed and Ward, as publishers, lived to see their ultimate goal accomplished: an American "dead-from-the-neck-up" church nourished and prodded out of the ghetto of the 1940's, 1950's and early 1960's by a loose confederation of European and home-grown movements and prophets called the Catholic Revival. Starring: Monsignor Ronald Knox, "the aging whiz kid of English Catholicism," the "flamboyant emigree," Baroness Catherine de Hueck and her interracial Harlem "Friendship House," which was torn asunder when a white woman wanted to marry a black; *Commonweal,* where Wilfrid served as book editor and drama critic, *Jubilee,* and *Integrity* with its Marycrest utopian farm experiment; Jacques Maritain, Thomas Merton, the young Hans Küng, Charles Davis (whom Wilfrid doesn't mention), Michael Quoist's "prayers of our time," and a "gnome" convert, Caryll Houselander, a spiritual writer who loved to talk with polio-stricken Wilfrid while she painted his portrait.

Much of this the boy Wilfrid observed silently from the sidelines, but he took mental notes and later started working his experiences into the novel manuscript he kept in his desk drawer. When Wilfrid was twelve, at Delbarton, the "eccentric" Benedictine school in Morristown, New Jersey, where most of the priests were, in Wilfrid's eyes, "inmates of a dumping ground," one of the few good teachers, Father Adrian, told him he was a "nice enough chap" when he was not writing, but then he "turned into a scorpion."

Indeed his pen does sting. He draws the glittering Monsignor Fulton J. Sheen, whom he worked for briefly, as "the plastic man, all style and no content," who "talked like a recording even when you were alone with him," and tended to plagiarize a bit in his books. And even Dorothy Day, a dear family friend, was in Frank's estimate only "eighty-five percent unphony," and perhaps a "little too theatrical."

For some critics, Sheed's wit has kidnaped his art. He does give his readers an average of three quips and one solid laugh a page, sometimes at the expense of an unfavorite institution, like his second Benedictine school, Downside, the "*reductio ad absurdum* of Englishness," and sometimes in just a clever observation, such as: in serving Benediction, "I got tangled up with the censer, a tiny tub of incense suspended by three wires which have to be pulled up and down in unison, like cables on an old French elevator, or all hell breaks loose."

Is his off-putting wit a refusal to deal deeply with pain or serious issues? Stricken with polio at thirteen, he'll take no pity from us nor from himself. He never asked, "Why me?" Rather, "Why not me? Who else would you suggest?" But confesses he would go "stark staring crazy" if one of his children got polio today.

Most likely Wilfrid is funny because he is his father's son. He once told John Updike that you were punished in his family if you weren't funny. Somehow, Frank and Maisie were non-stop fun, as delighted by the absurdities of human nature as by its glories. Just the other day I heard that one of Frank's favorite street-corner encounters was with a Hyde Park heckler who challenged the truth of the ascension on the grounds that if Jesus had ascended from Australia he would have had to take off upside down!

I inherited Wilfrid's old desk at *Commonweal* and met him occasionally at literary cocktail parties, and first met Frank at the publisher's celebration for *The Church and I*. I recall pretending not to notice Wilfrid's crutches or Frank's W.C. Fields nose, but now Wilfrid has mentioned both in his book. In the early chapters Wilfrid refers to Frank in the present tense, as if he were still alive, only to bring the reader up short on page 37 with the news that Frank has died as his son types away that November 20, 1982, telling the story of his father's life.

The last time I saw Frank he was making his way up the subway stairs in Greenwich Village, having braved the cold, wet night to come over from Jersey City, where he and Maisie had found cheaper housing in their last years, to preach at a memorial Mass in St. Joseph's Church for Dorothy Day, who had so often trudged over from Staten Island while Maisie was dying in 1975. The year I read this book I was living at St. Peter's College in their old neighborhood; the day I finished it, with tears in my eyes, I took a cold, gray afternoon run through Holy Name Cemetery at the bottom of our street—the closest thing to rural peace in this town of honking horns, ambulance sirens and cluttered gutters—and stopped at the single stone beneath which they both lie. Then as I jogged through the gate and up the hill to the college, I half expected to meet Frank and Maisie, talking and laughing, on the street.

V

The Private Lives
of Priests

21

Not Without Tears

GEORGE BERNANOS, *The Diary of a Country Priest*
(1936)

"How little we know what a human life really is—even our
own."

Every so often the story of a priest's death reminds us of how far
most people are from an intimate—even a proper—understanding of the personal turmoil—the struggle between the lighter and
darker shades of the self—that renders the emotional lives of
many priests a prolonged purgatory, if not an outright hell.

Sometimes, though rarely, a priest even kills himself—subject
to the same despair as someone who has never had the consolations of belief.

In Paris a distinguished theologian, a curial cardinal, once seen
as an intellectual liberal but now more famous for his rigid orthodoxy, is found dead at the foot of the stairway of a house in
the red light district. What brought him to that end and that
place? An errand of mercy? Some midnight acting out of a com-
pulsion so long held in check? In Brooklyn or Arizona a popular
parish priest ends up stabbed or bludgeoned to death in a seedy
motel room or the front seat of a car, victim of some secret inner
struggle as well as of some murdering hustler who has exploited
him.

One of the social functions of fiction is to make public the secret inner lives of men and women whose professions seem to
depend most strongly on those masks that make them mysteries

to the rest of us—to lay bare the souls of presidents, princes and priests. But literature in general—particularly popular best-selling fiction—has not done well in making the priest an understandable human being—perhaps because so few novelists know priests intimately, and perhaps because so few priests have the literary skills, indiscretion with the secrets of others, discipline and personal courage to become novelists.

The great French novelist George Bernanos had, he said, no more theological training than his catechism at the Jesuit school in Paris, and was the struggling father of six when he wrote to a friend in 1935 about his plan to write the diary of a country priest who "will have served God in exact proportion to his belief that he has served Him badly. His naiveté will win out in the end, and he will die peacefully of cancer."

So simple an outline of so complex a work—to which Bernanos brought, if not theology, a profound spirituality formed in steady dialogue with God since his youth, an obsession with the fear of death heightened by his battle experiences in World War I, his own suffering from illness and poverty, as well as his artistic vision.

Today readers may shrink from *The Diary of a Country Priest,* perhaps influenced by the stark images of the Robert Bresson film, because it is "gloomy." But, as Peter Hebblethwaite says, there is more joy in it "than a hasty first reading might suggest. But it is a hard-won joy, not excluding suffering and apparent failure. It is the paradox of the Beatitudes."

Through the ingenious diary form the reader both sees the young curé as the curé sees himself, foolish and inexperienced, stumbling and bumbling his way from one apparent failure to another as he makes his rounds of his country parish, and as he is—or as Bernanos would have us see him, the hero-saint, in the contemporary re-enactment of Christ's agony in the garden.

Through the diary we also learn what he calls "the very simple trivial secrets of a very ordinary kind of life"; share the priest's recollections of his own impoverished background; sense in him the makings of a poet, an intellectual with powers of analysis which will never come to fruition; and deal with the relatively limited but powerfully drawn group of characters who constitute his world.

In the Curé de Torcy, his older friend and spiritual mentor, we hear Bernanos' other voice, the monarchist, the realist, the man of a previous generation who, if he does not romanticize the medieval Church, at least longs for its unity, its vision of the well-ordered Christian society. He warns his young comrade: "A true priest is never loved, get that into your head. And if you must know, the Church doesn't care a rap whether you're loved or not, my lad. Try first to be respected and obeyed."

This "lad" does not ask for love; he only seeks to give it—by ministering to a corrupt village lorded over by a corrupt aristocracy in a chateau where the count is having an affair with the governess and the countess hates her adolescent daughter for surviving when the countess' son died in infancy. Meanwhile, the curé makes his rounds in constant pain—the cancer, which he mistakes for tuberculosis, eating away his stomach in the way that spiritual decay is eating away at France.

At the novel's climax the curé, with the fearless honesty that can come only from humility, confronts the countess, forces her to deal with her hatred, and brings her peace. But she dies of a heart attack that night. The daughter and the villagers spread rumors that the curé is a rash fool who turns the heads of young girls and drinks. Indeed, the curé is trapped by alcoholism, not from his indulgence, but rather from the tainted blood of his poor peasant family and his miserable diet of stale bread and foul wine. The curé dies in Lille where he has gone, much too late, to consult a specialist, and to visit a seminary friend who has left the priesthood.

Knowing he has not long to live, he stays up all night and pours himself into his diary. "I can understand how a man, sure of himself and his courage, might wish to make of his death a perfect end. As that isn't in my line, my death shall be what it can be, and nothing more. Were it not a very daring thing to say, I would like to add that to a true lover, the halting confession of his beloved is more dear than the most beautiful poem. And when you come to think of it, such a comparison should offend no one, for human agony is beyond all an act of love."

"God might possibly wish my death as some form of example to others. But I would rather have their pity. Why shouldn't I? I have loved men greatly, and I feel this world of living creatures has been so pleasant. I cannot go without tears."

22

The Cheerleader

EDWIN O'CONNOR, *The Edge of Sadness* (1961)

Edwin O'Connor, who died in Boston in 1968, when he was not yet fifty years old, is probably most familiar as the author of that warm, satirical, quintessentially 1956 Boston novel, *The Last Hurrah,* which affectionately chronicled the passing of the old mayor, Frank Skeffington, and his political establishment, to be replaced by something perhaps slightly more "clean" and certainly less colorful.

But the O'Connor novel which won the Pulitzer Prize in 1962, and which should endure, with the work of J.F. Powers, as long as fiction can illuminate the soul of American Catholicism, is *The Edge of Sadness.* It is so powerful and so accurate in its depiction of the American clerical subculture and of one fallible human being who is both its victim and its exemplar that I found myself almost praying at Mass for its hero as if he were a living priest in a parish down the street.

O'Connor does here for the Boston Irish Catholic what Thoreau proposed for the American individual—he drives life into a corner, reduces it to its lowest terms, and does not shrink from the "meanness" he discovers there. Yet, in O'Connor, this confrontation with the self in the corner is an occasion of grace, of salvation. Also, like George Bernanos, he has created a simple, weak and holy man who narrates his own story, and whose secret—his holiness—is often a secret from himself.

It is the story of a fifty-five year old Hugh Kennedy, once driven into depression, loneliness and alcoholism by his father's death, and now, after four years of therapy, a better, but still withdrawn, priest, pastor of a changing, crumbling parish—typical of a church, a city, and lives that are crumbling too.

He had begun his priesthood in a flurry of apostolic zeal, but had discovered, after neglecting his interior life for too long, that he had become nothing but a cheerleader in a Roman collar. Now he is simply marking time and passively behaving himself, allowing his bubbling young Polish curate to hustle around getting to know the people. Father Hugh is praying and not drinking—but not really living either.

Then one day his past breaks through his solitude: he accepts an invitation from the eighty-one year old Charlie Carmody, an old neighbor, a wealthy real estate operator and rent gouger, whom Hugh's father had once described as "as fine a man as ever robbed the helpless," to join his family at Charlie's birthday dinner.

It is an Irish family instantly recognizable to anyone who has attended alumni banquets and President's Club dinners at Boston College, Holy Cross or Fordham—an extended clan of four generations including: the tyranical, manipulative but wily chief; the long-suffering daughter Mary who stays home to care for him; another daughter, Helen, to whom Hugh feels close, but who is stuck in a barely tolerable marriage to a dull doctor; Father John the priest who loathes his parishioners; the blacksheep brother Dan, always trying to rope friends into a fast-buck scheme; and handsome, young grandson Ted all set to run for Congress. And each has his or her own story to pour into the weary ear of the fragile Father Hugh.

But Father Hugh, who had earlier desired little more than his own peace, now drawn into the lives and pain of this family, discovers in mid-life his almost snuffed-out power to empathize and to love.

And also to teach. In my favorite scene, young Ted, preparing his election campaign, stops in on Father Hugh, allegedly for priestly advice; but, as the conversation develops, it seems that candidate Ted is really interested in meeting the voters in the parish. In a line stunning in its insensitivity he blurts, "I could even break the ice, I imagine, by doing something like passing the basket at the collection at Mass—just so they'd have the feeling that I wasn't coming up cold to them on the church steps." Stung and disappointed, like any priest or teacher who discovers cynicism in the young, Father Hugh tells Ted about the distinction between ends and means, that the Mass is a prayer: "You can't *use* it for anything else."

Again, as in life, the novel's main moral crisis comes over a relatively minor matter. The apparently dying crank, old Carmody, aware that he is a hated old man but grasping for one sign of respect, asks Father Hugh what his father really thought of him.

As Father Hugh's story reaches its resolution, O'Connor has exposed the soul not just of a wounded Boston priest but of every man and woman, in mid-life, who is brave enough to face one's own weakness, then step back from the edge of self-pity, to use prayer for what it's meant for.

23

Lamb Among Lions

J.F. POWERS, *Morte D'Urban* (1962)

"I believe that the world will be saved by the poor," George Bernanos once wrote; and his poverty-stricken curé in *The Diary of A Country Priest* scribbled in his journal: "By nature I am probably coarse-grained, for I confess that I have always been repelled by the lettered priest. After all, to cultivate clever people is merely a way of dining out, and a priest has no right to go out to dinner in a world full of starving people."

I would be very surprised if J.F. Powers was not an admirer of Bernanos; but their priest characters move in very different circles. While the curé is soaking his hard bread in bad wine, Father Urban and a clerical pal are downing lamb and champagne in Chicago's Pump Room, and remarking that Jesus also ate lamb. Both Bernanos and Powers are concerned with the mediocrity that sets the tone of the Church's sub-culture—but for Powers' Father Urban, the fund-raiser for the Clementine Fathers, a religious order outstanding only in the pervasiveness of its mediocrity, poverty is more often the having to cope with the stupidity and shriveled imaginations of his peers.

No novelist has so meticulously—nor hilariously—described the daily doings inside the average American rectory or religious community of men: the housekeepers and cooks who rule and possess their charges more absolutely than many wives; the petty power struggles and jealousies over apostolic turf; the once cozy recreation room overcome by the new TV. While in these small worlds—seldom touched by the great social conflicts of race and war—the priests try, within the limitations of a disintegrating way of life, to lead holy—or at least good—lives.

Father Urban, "fifty-four, tall and handsome but a trifle loose in the jowls and red of eye," is a whiz, a spellbinder in the pulpit and at small town midwestern garden parties, the kind of popular priest who sees in every new face a soul to be saved and a potential benefactor to be cultivated—though not necessarily in that order. Sent in turn to a crumbling retreat house and a foundering parish, he revives one by building a golf course to attract a higher-class clientele and the other by conducting a census that demonstrates the need for a new church.

In one of the novel's funniest chapters, Urban plays golf with the bishop, a Presbyterian minister, and Father Feld, a stocky little champ whom the bishop has brought along to whip Urban in retaliation for trouncing the bishop a few months before. Urban has decided it will be good politics to allow the bishop his surrogate victory, until he sees the Clementine novices gathered on the hill to cheer him on. Another kind of Catholic novel gives the priest a more dramatic moral crisis—how to advise his unmarried sister who wants an abortion or whether to buy a papal election—but Powers sees integrity won and lost in little battles as well as grand.

The "death" Urban undergoes is the awful discovery that the line between himself and Sinclair Lewis' George Babbitt is a thin one. Urban has always argued that lambs can lie down with lions and live; but the shady businessman and rich widow he has pursued and pampered have brought him in their doors, bought him drinks and presents, and kept him there on their terms. The thirtyish rich woman who invites him for a nude midnight swim after drinks by the fireplace tells him: "You're an operator . . . and I don't think you have a friend in the world."

In 1966, writing in *America* on Crawford Power's reissued novel, *The Encounter,* about a Maryland priest who sees his own life mysteriously tied to a circus acrobat, I predicted that the "priest-novel for tomorrow's generation" would be written or inspired by the "movement"—"a priest student or seminarian who takes the Gospel so seriously that both the promise and corruption of modern society, the problems of race, peace and poverty, seem more than ever the priest's special province." It hasn't happened. The priest novels for today's and tomorrow's generation were written fifty and twenty-five years ago.

VI
Forming the Social Conscience

24

Never Again

ELIE WIESEL, *Night* (1958)

As we first approach Nathan Rappaport's 154-foot bronze statue, "Liberation," in Jersey City's Liberty State Park, set off against a panorama of the New York Harbor with the Statue of Liberty and the twin towers of the World Trade Center soaring in the background, we see in the human figures what we take for two GIs. A tall, erect, massive, stoic but compassionate young man in a World War II helmet cradles in his arms the body—alive or dead?—of a comrade, head hanging back limp, barefoot, shirt torn open to expose a bony chest, his bearer's huge hands holding his knee and torso.

But as we gaze up from beneath it we see that the victim is not an American GI. A star of David emblazons the open shirt and the dangling forearm is tattooed. The soldier is carrying a Jew from a concentration camp. Our first perception was wrong.

But then we realize that we were really not mistaken. We had perceived what the artist intended—a brother bearing a brother to freedom, the universal message of the holocaust embodied in two familiar human beings.

In an April 18, 1945 *New York Times* story, Gene Currivan describes how 1,200 German civilians were treated to a forced tour of the liberated Buchenwald to see the gallows, torture rooms, dissection rooms, crematoria, experimental laboratories, and stacks of naked corpses for which they had to bear, in some way, responsibility.

"The German people saw all this today, and they wept. Those

who didn't weep were ashamed. They said they didn't know about it, and maybe they didn't because the camp was restricted to Army personnel, but there it was right at their back doors for eight years."

By then 60,000 prisoners had been recently evacuated; but 32,705 had been murdered since 1937. One of the 20,000 prisoners rescued by the American forces on April 10 was a fifteen year old Jewish boy named Elie Wiesel who, in 1944, had been rounded up with his family in a Transylvanian ghetto and shipped first to Birkenau, then to Auschwitz, where Elie and his father lost his mother and sister forever, then to Buna, where, in despair, what was once his prayer became, "Blessed art Thou, Eternal Master of the Universe, Who chose us from among the races to be tortured day and night, to see our fathers, our mothers, our brothers, end in the crematory. . . ." He became God's accuser.

Too, this is the story of a son's battle to keep his father alive—until he is so exhausted that he finally feels freed by his father's death.

When Francois Mauriac, who believed that God is love, met Wiesel years later, he was tempted to tell him of that other Israeli, "his brother, who may have resembled him," whose suffering was the key to the mystery in which his childhood faith had perished. But he only embraced him, and wept.

25

The Curse of Nationalism

AMOS OZ, *In The Land Of Israel* (1983)

In July 1985, when I walked the winding streets of the Old City
of Jerusalem, where teenage Israeli militia men and women stroll
through the markets with their submachine guns, and jogged
around its walls, and when I drove south to Masada and the Dead
Sea and north through Arab territories captured during the 1967
six-day war to Nazareth and the Sea of Galilee, and south along
the Jordan to Jericho and past the new Israeli settlements on desert
hilltops on the road back to Jerusalem, my intellectual compan-
ion was novelist-journalist Amos Oz's account of his own listening tour of his homeland.

A Zionist who fought in both the 1967 war and the Yom Kip-
pur war of 1973, Oz now worries about the moral damage that
these victories have done to the victors.

Nationalism, in his eyes, is the curse of mankind, and he fears
that there are political forces at work in Israel that, by advocating
the annexation of Judea and Samaria, may turn it into a "monster
like Belfast, Rhodesia, or South Africa."

Oz sees Judaism as a civilization that is nourished by the union
of Jewish tradition and Western humanism, which means, in a
nutshell, "the absolute sanctity of the life and liberty of the individual. It is justice and 'do not do unto others what you would
not have others do unto you' within a universal framework, not
just a Jewish-tribalistic framework."

Like any great writer, Oz is a great listener, and he gives his
political and religious critics—in the newspaper pieces which are

the basis of this book—plenty of space to tear him apart; but he absorbs their verbal violence. He also gives a beautiful chapter to the wisdom of a French priest, Father Marcel Dubois, head of the philosophy department of the Hebrew University of Israel, who reminds his listener, and us, of God's special love for Israel and the need for all who love it to pray "for its triumph in the struggle—for its triumph over itself."

26

Two Visits To Christie Street

MICHAEL HARRINGTON, *The Other America* (1962, 1971, 1981)

"I am a pious apostate, an atheist shocked by the faithlessness of the believers, a fellow traveler of moderate Catholicism who has been out of the church for more than twenty years." So begins *Fragments of a Century,* Michael Harrington's personal memoir of the 1950's and 1960's. He declares himself a product of the middle class Irish Catholic ghettos of St. Louis and Holy Cross College, where the intellectual decadence of rationalistic neo-Thomism, which forgot the complexity of the human soul, began to sour him on Catholicism.

Yet in 1971 he received a Holy Cross honorary degree and gave the graduation address. Many of those who have admired Harrington's books and journalism for years still think of him as part of the Catholic tradition—perhaps because some elements of the faith are so deep in his bones that today his economic and political values seem steeped in Christian principles absorbed in his years living and working at the Catholic Worker House of Hospitality on Skid Row in 1951 and 1952. There he read the breviary daily, and daily came face to face with the down-and-out poor who were to become the subject of *The Other America: Poverty in the United States,* one of the most influential books in modern American history.

He defined poverty in terms of "those who are denied the minimal levels of health, housing, food and education that our present stage of scientific knowledge specifies for life as it is now lived in the United States." His dividing line, following the Bureau of Labor Statistics, was $4,000 a year for a family of four and $2,000 for an individual living alone. This meant that between forty and fifty million Americans, or about a fourth of the population, were poor—really hard put to get enough to eat. Then he went on to explain how the poor had become "invisible." The fact that good clothes were cheap hid the fact that those wearing them were not decently housed, fed or doctored. Over 8,000,000 of the poor were over sixty-five years of age, many sitting alone in rented rooms, many without phones, and suffering from mental illness. The young poor were confined to their ghettos—sometimes advertising their poverty through a lurid tabloid headline about a gang killing.

Most of the poor he described were from large, established cultures of poverty—migrant farmworkers; the big city economic underclass of dishwashers and laundry workers not covered by the 1961 Minimum Wage Law and earning about $45.50 a week; Appalachians no longer needed in the mines and farmers incapable of competing with the mechanized agribusiness of the Midwest; and blacks doubly impoverished by being born into the institutionalized consequences of color. But Harrington also introduced us to three other subcultures of poverty: the bohemian intellectual, the rural poor who had migrated to the cities, and the alcoholics he came to know on Christie Street working with Dorothy Day.

The Other America, at first little noticed, had the good luck to inspire a long review by Dwight Macdonald in *The New Yorker,* which was reprinted as a pamphlet. Through the conversations the review touched off in the intellectual Northeast, the book reached John F. Kennedy, who decided to make poverty a central issue in his next presidential campaign. Lyndon Johnson continued this commitment in his War on Poverty, a war which made some progress, but which became another casualty of the other war in Vietnam.

After several editions in which he updated *The Other America* for the 1970's and 1980's, and after many other books, Harrington finally produced a sequel, *The New American Poverty* (1984), in which he measures the progress made—particularly in public awareness of the poor—but warns that one of today's problems is not so much ignorant indifference as a sophisticated and "scientific" attempt by some political leaders to define the poor out of existence. The poverty of the 1980's, he says, is different from all those poverties that preceded it—internationalized, "feminized," more violent than ever in the blood of drug wars.

In a sad chapter of the new book he returns to his old Bowery haunts where he had lived at the Worker thirty years before, only to find the old Bowery gone. Even the Catholic Worker had locked the door! Before, the door was always open and anyone could walk in. But now the drifter population is more young and angry. There are fights in the food line, tension between blacks, Hispanics and Anglos. The "homeless," many of them mental patients, can get nasty and violent. "Even the followers of St. Francis of Assisi must bolt the door."

One of the considerable strengths of Harrington's writings is that he invites his readers to not rest with what they have read, but to take a walk and explore the neighborhoods of their home towns where the poor live.

One of the considerable strengths of the American bishops' pastoral letter on *Catholic Social Teaching and the U.S. Economy* is that the document was developed through years of dialogue, both within the American church and between the bishops and a great range of religious and secular authorities, and reflects a broad understanding of the realities Harrington describes.

Almost as if its drafters had taken some of those walks and seen, as I often saw as I took my long runs through the poorest neighborhoods of Jersey City, the unemployed men and boys on the street corners outside the bars, lingering aimlessly—or one time rolling around on the sidewalk with four cops who were putting cuffs on them—tossing their bottle caps into the street where, over the years, they have become imbedded by the thousands, symbols of the dead lives of the men who throw them away.

The letter makes three moral points that its readers are left to consider and make their own. (1) Economic ideas have human consequences: the promotion of human dignity is the primary criterion for evaluating every social institution. (2) The resources of the world—natural and economic—are given to us by God in *stewardship* to be used and preserved for the whole human race. (3) The moral function of government is to secure basic justice for all citizens.

I would be surprised if our "pious apostate" socialist author was not very much at home with those ideas.

27

Everybody Should Have
Something To Point To

Studs Terkel, *Working* (1974)

The American bishops' pastoral letter on *Catholic Social Teaching and the U.S. Economy,* in its long and sometimes controversial analysis of the successes and failures of the American Dream, also attempts to revive a respect for the dignity of work.

For the Christian, especially the educated Christian familiar with the monastic tradition wherein to work is to pray, or one influenced by the Teilhardian notion that each of us contributes to the gradual spiritualization of matter by sharing in the ongoing work of creation, work is one of the highest forms of self-expression. As the bishops' letter states, all work has a threefold moral significance: human self-expression and self-realization; the fulfillment of material needs; its contribution to the well-being of the community.

But to a great many Americans, perhaps most, those ideas are foreign, if not laughable.

And a bitter laughter at that. Work is an ordeal. Period. A third to a half of a day of pain and boredom completely isolated from any statement of who the worker is or hopes to be.

Studs Terkel's book, *Working,* shows through extraordinary interviews made over three years with workers themselves—nearly all otherwise "inarticulate" citizens, men and women in jobs that give them no opportunity to talk to an audience about what they do—that work is "violence—to the spirit as well as to the body." It is ulcers, accidents, fist fights, nervous breakdowns and humiliations.

There are only a few good listeners in the world and Terkel, a Chicago radio interviewer and writer, is one of them. He kicks the tape recorder alongside him and cusses it to assure his subject it's a harmless piece of technology. So they talk. In a series of books like *Division Street: America,* about the destruction of Jane Addams' Hull House; *Hard Times,* on the Depression; and *The Good War,* on World War II, he has allowed hundreds of the faceless and voiceless to escape the anonymity that characterizes their condition, to become immortalized in print.

In this way he has become many things: a unique journalist, a social historian who documents what the daily lives of twentieth century American men and women are really like, and a guardian and interpreter of the American Dream.

Mike LeFevre, a thirty-seven year old steelworker in Cicero, Illinois, is one of a "dying breed." "Strictly muscle work . . . pick it up, put it down, pick it up, put it down. . . . You can't take pride anymore." He would like to see on the Empire State Building "a foot-wide strip from top to bottom with the name of every bricklayer, the name of every electrician, with all the names. So when a guy walked by, he could take his son and say, 'See, that's me over there on the forty-fourth floor. I put the steel beam in.' . . . Everybody should have something to point to."

Roberta Victor has been a prostitute since she was fifteen. "You become your job. I became what I did. I became a hustler. I became cold, I became hard, I became turned off, I became numb. Even when I wasn't hustling, I was a hustler. I don't think it's terribly different from somebody who works on the assembly line forty hours a week and comes home cut off, numb, dehumanized. People aren't built to switch on and off like water faucets."

For Maggie Holmes, a black domestic, work is being told by a suburban housewife to get down and clean the floor on her knees, since the house, allegedly, has no mop.

For sixty-two year old Louis Hayward, the washroom attendant at Chicago's Palmer House, who always wanted to be a writer, work means forking over to the Mafia twenty-five cents on every two towels handed out.

Most of the stories are bad, powerful documentation of human beings being broken by their jobs. Terkel is a liberal who has a strong sense that there is something wrong with an economic system that leaves so many people poor and so many rich people spiritually impoverished. But he has the liberal's trust in and love for human beings. His last three interviews are with Harold Patrick, a socialist elevator operator, and his two sons.

Bob, a Brooklyn ghetto policeman, is afraid that after seeing so much evil and suffering he will lose his ability to feel: "I hope to God it never happens. I hope to God I always feel."

His brother Tom is a fireman: "The thing is you gotta like people. If you like people, you have a good time with 'em." Tom has the last line of the book: "But I can look back and say, 'I helped put out a fire. I helped save somebody.' It shows something I did on this earth."

28

City On A Hill

J. ANTHONY LUKAS, *Common Ground: A Turbulent Decade in the Lives of Three American Families* (1985)

Over the last twenty years—beginning perhaps with the publication of John Howard Griffin's *Black Like Me* (1961) and followed soon by James Baldwin's *The Fire Next Time* (1963)—the average thoughtful white liberal Christian, the reader to whom J. Anthony Lukas' *Common Ground* has the most to say, has gone through a distinct series of emotional stages on the issue of race.

Guilt: the white community's realization of its responsibility for the black race's poverty and oppression. *Commitment:* marches and demonstrations, support for civil rights legislation, integrated and subsidized housing. *Romance:* uncritical co-option—black theology, black studies, Black Panthers, Black Power! *Confusion:* black "ingratitude," no visible progress. *Rage:* muggings, junkies, housing projects as "jungles," graffiti and "ghetto blasters" on subways and streets.

In short, the man who wept to hear Martin Luther King's "I have a dream" speech now feels a guilty twinge of satisfaction when Bernhard Goetz shoots three black youths who threaten him on the subway.

To read *Common Ground,* the story of busing in Boston, slowly and painfully, is to experience not just all those emotions again, but a great many other emotions as well—above all the frustration, abandonment and rage of the black poor and the middle and lower-class Irish who—depending on their points of view—were either struggling for educational rights or made victims of a Quixotic social experiment.

The story begins with Colin Diver, a smart Harvard Law School grad who, moved by the assassination of Martin Luther King, passes up a job at a leading Washington law firm to join the staff of Boston's exciting new mayor, Kevin White, who has vowed to make Boston a truly integrated city. In the same spirit, he moves his wife and two children into an 1865 brick town house in the South End, a mixed neighborhood in the inner city. The story ends as Diver breaks a baseball bat over the head of a Puerto Rican mugger, then moves to the wealthy suburb of Newton and surrounds his clapboard house with a white picket fence.

But if the Divers frame the story they are not necessarily its focus; indeed, rather than give a point of view, Lukas recreates the history of Boston, between the riots following King's assassination in 1968 and the bloody back-street neighborhood busing wars of the Bicentennial summer, through eight perspectives, three families and five public figures.

Each story reaches back to its roots in Africa or Ireland, then marches up through the black or Irish ghettos or wilderness of the New World, where one person might end up a rich Yankee snob, a whining bigot, a power-grubbing politician, a reforming idealist, a crook, a suffering mother, a hand-wringing priest or some combination of them all.

As the saga unfolds, Lukas lets both the events and characters—all real—speak for themselves, and leaves us not with the truth about the rightness of the 1973 decision of Federal Court Judge W. Arthur Garrity that the Boston School Committee had "knowingly carried out a systematic program of segregation affecting all of the city's students, teachers and school facilities," and the 1974 busing plan which he imposed and administered to overcome racial imbalance, but the community experience itself. And if in the process, for the reader, moral clarity fades, moral wisdom gains.

Between 1940 and 1960 Boston's black population mushroomed from 23,675 to 63,165, the swarm of Cotton Belt South-

erners shattering the "special relationship" some of the minority
had enjoyed with the city's establishment. By 1970 blacks were
16.4 percent of the city's population—not much compared to
other cities, and if one kept to one's "own" neighborhood, blacks
were relatively invisible. Even today a visitor can join the evening throngs at the magnificent Quincy Market development of
shops and restaurants near City Hall and seldom see a black face.
So, the fate of the Twymon family is central to the book.

Rachel Twymon, suffering from lupus, on welfare, burdened
with six children—two from a boyfriend, four from a drunken
bum she had jailed—lives in a hideous project a few blocks from
the Divers. She supports the busing of her daughters across town
to Charlestown—whose inhabitants are known as "Townies"—
on Bunker Hill because, as she tells them, "You're going to be
spat at, maybe pushed around some. But it's not the first time
this has happened and it won't be the last. It's something we have
to go through—something you have to go through—if this city
is ever going to get integrated." But the daughters end up hanging out on the street instead of studying, and one son is jailed for
rape.

Kevin White's wife comes from Charlestown, but her family
is from "the top of the hill." Alice McGoff is not. Her bartender
husband dies at thirty-seven, leaving her seven children to raise
in a shabby Bunker Hill housing project and in a pervasive sub-
culture of free-floating rage and grievance that, Lukas says, clung
to the town's "hills and valleys just as the coastal fog wrapped its
rotting wharves at dawn."

The McGoffs and their fellow tribesmen and women greet the
Twymons with a resistance that they call a defense of their community and the outside world calls violence and bigotry. Furthermore, their religion fortifies their resistance as the women
parade the streets chanting Hail Marys as an incantation to ward
off intruding blacks.

Meanwhile, as the busses shuttle back and forth amid showers
of stones and bottles, as students pass through metal detectors,
stage sit-ins and boycotts and exchange shoves and insults in the
corridors, as the teachers in what appears to be one of the worst

public school systems in the country either reinforce the bigotry of their pupils or try to overcome it, the city's power people manipulate the crisis or strive fitfully to contain it.

Louise Day Hicks, chairwoman of the school committee, has opposition to busing make her a candidate for mayor. Mayor Kevin White, distracted by his ambition to be governor or president, backs away from the racial issue and ends up a nervous wreck, done in by a need to consolidate his power.

Tom Winship, new editor of the *Boston Globe,* wins a Pulitzer Prize for busing coverage—partly by playing down the bad news—and turns the *Globe* into a leading national paper.

Cardinal Madeiros, humble and pious, frozen out by narrow-minded local clergy, burdened by a huge debt inherited from the beloved but erratic Cardinal Cushing, intimidated by Boston bullies, never rises to the challenge to bring the Church's full clout to bear on race.

A few years ago I met Judge Garrity at a Holy Cross College dinner—for only a few seconds, but long enough to express my admiration. *Common Ground* offers nothing to weaken and much to shore up that admiration; and if the book has a moral center it is he.

Lukas attributes that unique moral sense to Garrity's Holy Cross education in that "relentlessly logical discipline," Thomistic natural law philosophy, which bases natural rights on divine law. To his critics, Garrity is a Kennedy lieutenant, an aloof Puritan absolutist who lives in Wellesley, free from the consequences of his policies on ordinary people.

But regardless of the flaws in the busing plan itself, Garrity emerges as a man of integrity who suffers social ostracism and death threats in order to enforce the law. Garrity would have preferred desegregation without busing. But there was no other way. In this sense, his decision echoes to the white community Rachel Twymon's words to her children: it is something we have to go through.

Today Boston, to the visitor, dazzles with its new skyscrapers and chic downtown neighborhoods swarming with Young Upwardly-mobile Urban Professionals. But the schools are predominantly black—as the *Washington Post* reports, a place "for people who can't afford to go elsewhere." Yet there is evidence that the races are learning to live together.

I suggest that *Common Ground* speaks particularly to Christians because they are the main actors in this story. Their faith either gives them moral strength, as with Rachel Twymon and Judge Garrity, or helps them avoid a real moral issue, as with Mrs. Hicks and the McGoffs, or offers a grace somehow never comprehended—as with some clergy.

On one level, *Common Ground* is an ironic title, a reminder that Americans are divided by class as much as race. On another level it is a challenge, particularly to those white Christians who have held political, social, economic and religious power in American cities since the Puritans and slaves arrived, a reminder and warning that the justice of the biblical "City on a Hill" our ancestors sought is still far beyond our grasp.

29

Remembering Vietnam

DAVID HALBERSTAM, *The Best And The Brightest*
   (1972)
WILLIAM SHAWCROSS, *Sideshow* (1979)

There is a danger that Vietnam may become the forgotten war.
True, there are many things about wars we should forget, such
as the propaganda that taught us to depersonalize and hate our
enemies, and any bitterness over wounds and losses that would
make it harder to forgive or to enter new relationships—humanitarian or economic—with people we once fought.

   But Vietnam was the one time in modern history where
America got a sense that America itself, as a collectivity, in its
policy or in the implementation of that policy, was wrong—
morally wrong.

   The awareness grew slowly across the country, beginning
with the traditional peace groups—like the Catholic Worker, the
Quakers, the Fellowship of Reconciliation—and spreading
among the draft-age young and their teachers, finally reaching
the political leaders, coming to a head with the campaigns of Sen-
ators Eugene McCarthy and Robert F. Kennedy in 1968.

   Perhaps as succinct a statement as could be made of the moral
argument against the war was a column by Anthony Lewis in the
New York Times during the 1972 presidential election campaign,
addressed to a college senior who had argued that students in a
religious school should "protect our investment" and support the
government's conduct of the war. Lewis replied that what was
involved was "not just an investment but human souls—Indo-

chinese more than Americans." In the last four years alone, two million people had been killed or wounded in the four little countries of Indochina. In South Vietnam a third of the population had been uprooted. Only we used B-52s in mass bombings of the North, including attacks on civilian targets; only we had offshore cruisers and destroyers bombarding unseen targets on land; only we sprayed massive doses of herbicide over the countryside and poured napalm on peasant villages. We were conducting a war of terror that was escalating the horror of the war between the Vietnamese and wounding the American character.

In a 1967 anthology, *Letters from Vietnam,* one boy wrote a sentence that revealed how much the generation in uniform in the jungles was one in spirit with the generation at home: "Every day I pray for only two things—to be out of this hell and back home, or to be killed before I might have to kill someone."

So we should not completely forget Vietnam for the same reasons that we should not forget the Last Supper and crucifixion, or the genocide of the Armenians or the Jews. We must find some way of rationally making both its stories of heroism and the record of national folly part of our common self-understanding.

Of the whole library shelf of books that will help us do this, two stand out.

David Halberstam's *The Best and The Brightest* depicts how an unsure and inexperienced President Kennedy fell back for direction on the old foreign policy establishment, and on the Whiz Kid, can-do, tough attitude of his businessman Secretary of Defense Robert McNamara. This team, which froze out differing opinions, pursued the war as if it were an abstract problem on a blackboard in a business school, with no regard for the human beings who were actually engaged in it. For this management elite, it was a game to be won by applying another dose of discipline, will power—and fire power.

With a novelist's skills, Halberstam, who covered the war for the *New York Times,* presents an 800-page picture of *hubris* egged on by *machismo*. Its ultimate and long-lasting effect on the reading public has been to undermine the once-deep confidence that

Americans had that their leaders—since they were the "best and the brightest"—could be trusted to do the right thing.

Although Saigon fell in 1975, the war has continued in Cambodia to the present day. Today Cambodia, invaded by the Vietnamese, who drove out the murderous Khmer Rouge in 1979, must be the most miserable place on earth. Between 1970 and 1980 it lost a third of its population to war and famine.

To an extent, the 1969 secret bombing of and 1970 incursion into Cambodia, which brought the anti-war protests to their highest pitch and precipitated the campus demonstrations that led to the killings at Kent State, was a "sideshow" to the larger conflict. Yet, as William Shawcross' book, *Sideshow,* makes clear—and the subsequent history of Cambodia has demonstrated as well—the story illustrates both why we cannot blindly trust our government and how much the human species, represented by any government, is always capable of cruelty on a scale not previously imagined.

Sideshow is a tale of unmitigated cruelty: the cruelty of the Khmer Rouge soldiers (mostly teenagers) who chop up and disembowel their enemies and display their severed heads on a table; and the cruelty of American policymakers—Nixon and Kissinger—who could not see their victims but—acting out the Nixon "madman theory of war" (calculated to keep opponents off balance) and dedicated to the mystique of bombing as a show of manly strength—carried out the secret and illegal bombing and disastrous invasion that brought on Cambodia's internal collapse.

Nixon and Kissinger have told their side of these events in their books, and anyone who doubts Shawcross' conclusions can read more widely, especially in Seymour Hersh's book on Kissinger, *The Price of Power.*

Meanwhile, the initially dispassionate reader of *Sideshow* will come to agree, at least emotionally, with Congressman Pete McCloskey, who said after a 1975 visit to Phnom Penh, "If I could have found the military or State Department leader who has been the architect of this policy, my instinct would be to string him up . . . what they have done to the country is greater evil than we have done to any country in the world, and wholly without reason, except for our own benefit to fight the Vietnamese."

As we know, those responsible have not been strung up. One leaves his Saddle River, New Jersey, estate from time to time to speak on foreign policy. The other received a medal as an outstanding "immigrant" at the 1986 celebration for the Statue of Liberty.

I realize that the decision to keep talking about Vietnam and Cambodia and American guilt for war crimes all depends on how we view history: whether we believe humanity can give a purposeful pattern to events, redress the balance between moral chaos and order by bringing the Nazi butchers before the tribunal at Nuremberg, or mitigate the holocaust of Nagasaki by rebuilding Japan, or purge out long collective acquiesence to violence by mass mourning before the TV screen as the Kennedy funeral train rumbles by.

If history is not cumulative and has no direction, and if our collective pasts do not constitute a national self that determines what we can do tomorrow, we can let Vietnam go. It is as gone as last summer's bird song.

I realize too that this approach accepts what more radical critics would deny, that the American nation is an organic whole, not unlike a human personality, with deep spiritual resources, the deepest of which is respect—based on humanitarianism and Christian theology—for human rights and the dignity of every individual. If our civilization is still at such a primitive stage that we have no culture, no strong common values—even on the absolute value of human life—and if we are not a nation but a patchwork alliance of ethnic and economic subcultures still scratching for security and power, we had best leave the memory of Vietnam alone.

VII

What Future For Humankind?

30

Replanting Eden

WALTER M. MILLER, JR., *A Canticle For Leibowitz*
(1957)

Almost any year is a good year to reread a good book, but *A Canticle for Leibowitz,* which, when it first appeared at the height of the Cold War when people were talking about bomb shelters in their back yards, drew comparisons with *Brave New World* and *1984* and *On the Beach,* seems to have grown in stature and impact with each republication and each day's headlines.

Its last chapter poses the question about the future of humankind in space: What good would it do to transplant our civilization, several times destroyed by nuclear wars and half-rebuilt, to another world where we would probably not let it survive? Since 1957 we have transplanted human hearts, photographed Mars up close, waged and lost the Vietnam War, created "life" in test tubes, come to the brink of several nuclear melt-downs, and watched a space shuttle blow up on TV. With this behind us, we should be all the more ready for what Walter M. Miller, Jr. has to say.

While some critics faulted *Canticle* for being "too Catholic," and others ignored it, the paperback—with a seared monk on its cover, transfigured against the blazing wreckage of civilization—has passed from friend to friend. Now it can be read not just as a piece of brilliant science fiction warning about the coming nuclear deluge, but as an underground sub-Scripture classic, an ethical tract.

The story begins a thousand years from now and spans seventy generations. The world is in ruins, reduced to barbarism by an accidental atomic war. In their Utah desert sanctuary, the monks of the Abbey of Blessed Leibowitz preserve the memorabilia, the last vestiges of human knowledge. Their blessed founder had been an electrical technician until his wife had been killed by fallout. Then he had instituted a religious order of copyists and memorizers to rescue human culture from the new Dark Ages. But Leibowitz had been martyred by the tribe of Simpletons—those who, seeing the havoc wrought by technology, feared a new renaissance.

Ironically, as centuries pass and man regains mastery over nature, the split between church and secular culture widens. Secular rulers and scientists again turn science and weapons into gods. The faith, as personified by each generation of monastery abbots, becomes the increasingly isolated conscience of mankind. When monsters, genetic victims of radiation, are born, the church alone demands that they be allowed to live. At the end of the book, when another Flame Deluge is turning cities into puddles of glass and piling up corpses by the millions, the last abbot spends his last breaths confronting the government Mercy Cadres, who would administer the secular sacrament of euthanasia to the dying.

Miller's church of the future, which will protect itself against the gates of hell by sending a spaceship full of monk-scientists, children, nuns and bishops (to preserve the apostolic succession) to another galaxy, retains, with all its learning, some of the worst aspects of the pre-conciliar church. Before the ship takes off, a monk slams the door and quips, "*Sic transit mundus!*" New Rome deals with its friends and foes by concordats and interdicts, as if old Rome had learned nothing from history. As the intercontinental missiles leave their launching pads in the war between the Atlantic and Asian states, the Pope stops praying for peace and sings the Mass in Time of War. In his conflict with the secular-humanist doctor who would put radiation victims out of their misery, the abbot can only reply with the Stoic dictum that nature imposes nothing on man that it doesn't prepare man to bear.

Yet the author of *Canticle* can hardly be expected to solve the problem of evil. It is enough that he suggests that we will never be able to replant Eden because we would never give it a chance to grow. We are like the children in *Lord of the Flies:* even when we are rescued from the primitive barbarism we have created on a tropical island, we are brought into a larger context of sophisticated barbarism in war.

Of course, since 1957 the church has changed. In what Msgr. Vincent A. Yzermans, in a *New York Times* article, called "the most significant revolution within the American Catholic Church since Lord Baltimore's contingent of Catholics disembarked on Maryland's shores in 1634," the "official" church, if not all the communicants, has started to become a "peace" church, especially with the publication of the American bishops' pastoral letter on disarmament, *The Challenge of Peace,* in 1982.

Also, since *Canticle* first appeared some new expressions—like Three Mile Island, Bhopal, *Challenger* and Chernobyl—have entered the language with their own warnings about our limited ability to control our technology and our fate. It may be that the memory of these events and the impact of the bishops' pastoral will fade. It may also be that more Americans have been able to comprehend these events because so many passed *Canticle* from friend to friend.

31

Requiem Or Hymn?

JONATHAN SCHELL, *The Fate of the Earth* (1982)

In August 1985, on my first evening in Vienna, I hurried up the grand stairway of the Opera House, while thousands gathered in the square outside to see and hear the music on a movie-theater-size TV screen, with the last seat for a concert called "Journey for Peace," the Hiroshima Peace Concert—Beethoven's "Leonore" Overture No. 3 and Fumiko Kohjiba's "Hiroshima Requiem," Mozart's Violin Concerto No. 5, and Leonard Bernstein's Symphony No. 3, "Kaddish"—with Leonard Bernstein and Eiji Oue conducting. The orchestra was the European Community Orchestra—young people, some teenagers, drawn from all over Europe to express their unity in their art.

The concert marked the end of Hiroshima Week, the fortieth anniversary of the days on which, as Radio Moscow and Radio Warsaw reminded us daily in their short-wave newscasts, the United States of America dropped the atom bombs on Hiroshima and Nagasaki. So, after Bernstein whipped and leaped and danced his youths through a triumphant "Leonore"—as thrilling a hymn to mankind's free spirit as we know—and rewarded them with hugs and kisses, Oue, born in Hiroshima in 1957, conducted the "Requiem," a stirring, mournful piece; and little Mi Dori, born in Osaka in 1971, did the Mozart, softly, hunched over, leaning into it, to the standing ovation she has been receiving for years.

It occurred to me that these young performers were both our shame and our hope: born twelve years after the bomb, did the smiling, cherubic Oue carry the effects of our radiation in his system? But were not the combined brilliance of Oue and Dori lyric testimony that one generation can somehow assimilate history's genius and outlive its crimes? And the young musicians in the orchestra: how do they differ from their brothers and sisters at Holy Cross, Fordham, Loyola, or St. Peter's College—or at American secular or state institutions—when they hear of the holocaust and the bomb?

That night in Vienna comes back to me when I read the books of Jonathan Schell.

Schell begins *The Abolition,* his sequel to *The Fate of the Earth,* with a quote from Pope John Paul II's speech in Hiroshima in February 1981: "In the past, it was possible to destroy a village, a town, a region, even a country. Now it is the whole planet that has come under a threat. This fact should fully compel everyone to face a basic moral consideration: from now on, it is only through a conscious choice and then deliberate policy that humanity can survive."

Schell's use of the Pope's speech is typical of his writing—not because he invokes a religious authority to fortify his arguments, but rather because his worldview, his value system, is one which religiously committed persons should share in an age when nuclear war could literally mean the end of the human species. His work is, borrowing from a combination of strategic and Christian terminology, a call for a policy of "preemptive repentance." We must repent the crime—of extinguishing the species by using nuclear weapons—before we commit it, and in that repentance find the will not to commit it. To him the only acceptable policy of deterrence is what he calls moral deterrence, in which we are deterred by the realization of what we would do to the enemy— "and to countless innocents, including all potential future generations of human beings."

I will not pretend that Schell's books have received complete critical acceptance, even among those who favor arms limitations. Theodore Draper, in *The New York Review of Books,* calls *The Fate of the Earth* "political fantasy and millennial daydreaming," and a "disguised counsel of despair." In Draper's judgment, Schell has drawn his conclusions from a worst-case scenario, whereas it might be that we could survive a first strike. Others might support the argument in Leon Wieseltier's *Nuclear War, Nuclear Peace,* which criticizes the extreme positions of what he calls the war party and peace party, and concludes that "freedom's immediate future" lies with the "party of deterrence." So it is best to read Schell and his critics, and see *The Abolition* as his response to questions raised after *The Fate of the Earth.*

Few books have been more successful in alerting the public to the effects of nuclear war and forcing a radical rethinking of nuclear policy than *The Fate of the Earth.* It is, in many ways, the *Uncle Tom's Cabin* of the anti-nuclear movement. When it first appeared in three issues of *The New Yorker,* readers were stunned by the implications of Schell's analysis, and moved to pass the articles, then the book, to their friends, strengthening what Schell calls, in *The Abolition,* the "new peace movement," the climate of opinion that will, in time, challenge the conventional wisdom that, no matter what, nuclear weapons are here to stay.

In *The Fate of the Earth* Schell does three things. (1) He describes in detail the nature of a nuclear explosion and its five distinctive effects: "initial nuclear radiation"; the electromagnetic pulse generated by gamma radiation which could destroy communications systems; the wave of blinding light and intense heat; the blast wave which flattens buildings; radioactive fallout. In doing so he demonstrates convincingly that the United States could not survive a nuclear attack by the Soviet Union. Indeed, the human species would not survive a nuclear war. (2) Drawing on philosophy, literature, art, and theology, Schell explains the historical and metaphysical unity of the human species—dead, living and yet-to-be-born. We are all parents of the future—of generations that will never exist if our love for humans, for the earth and for God is not strong enough to break through our current attitudes. (3) He demonstrates the logical and moral failure of deterrence as a strategy. Briefly: it is immoral to threaten to do what we cannot morally do. It would be immoral to use nuclear weapons first. And once we have been attacked, to retaliate would merely be an act of revenge, an insane action that would multiply the destruction already inflicted on the globe, kill millions of innocent people and likely render the planet unfit for habitation.

In Schell's view, if deterrence fails to prevent a nuclear attack, the only rational response is "to get on the hot line and try to stop the whole debacle as soon as possible." Obviously, any writer who says that the response to a nuclear attack should be a presidential phone call is not going to win wide acceptance in America today—even if he's right.

As Ivan Eisenberg pointed out, commenting on Schell in a provocative article in the *Nation* on the influence of the threat of a nuclear holocaust on music, what used to give death meaning was the continuity of mankind, and now that is in question. In "Late Night Thoughts on Listening to Mahler's Ninth Symphony," the biologist Lewis Thomas says that he once took Mahler's final movement as a tranquil reassurance that death was a peaceful experience. He had once thought of the earth as one organism, renewed in its cycle of living and dying. Now, with what he knows about the various weapons systems capable of destroying the life of any continent, he envisions the actual end of humanity itself. "I cannot hear the same Mahler. Now, those cellos sound in my mind like the opening of all the hatches and the instant before ignition." Since these books appeared, the nuclear accident at Chernobyl has demonstrated tragically and forcefully the validity of these themes: the utter inability of our medical resources to respond adequately to a nuclear attack; the common fate—and, we hope, brotherhood—that binds all nations for as long as the future will last.

32

Reasons for Living and Hope

PIERRE TEILHARD DE CHARDIN, S.J., *The Divine Milieu* (1957, 1960)

"The look in his eyes when they met your eyes revealed the man's soul. His reassuring sympathy restored your confidence in yourself." So writes Pierre LeRoy, S.J., about his friend Pierre Teilhard de Chardin in his introduction to Teilhard's *Letters from a Traveler.* In a sense, the "reassuring sympathy" of his personal presence sums up his intellectual impact on many thousands of readers—a sympathy for the world joined to a reassuring vision of the ultimate spiritual destiny of humanity and the material universe.

Born in 1881, a stretcher-bearer in World War I, Jesuit, traveler and paleontologist, co-discoverer of the Peking Man, Teilhard fused in his spirituality Christian salvation history and Darwinian evolution. Forbidden by religious superiors to publish his major works, *The Phenomenon of Man* and *The Divine Milieu,* both written in the 1920's, he suffered greatly, almost to despair, but continued to study and write. It is an irony of intellectual history that after his death his books finally burst upon America in the *milieu* most ready to absorb them—the 1960's.

His insistence that Catholics find their "rejuvenation" in "the perception of a more intimate connection between the victory of Christ and the outcome of the work which our human effort here below is seeking to construct" finds an echo in the last line of John F. Kennedy's inaugural address, "Here on earth God's work must truly be our own." Thus a generation on the brink of unprecedented technological change, as well as on the eve of Vatican II, was ready for a prophet-mystic who realized long before what the council finally said in the Pastoral Constitution on the Church in the Modern World: "The future of humanity lies in the hands of those who are strong enough to provide coming generations with reasons for living and hope."

As Thomas M. King, S.J. wrote in *America,* "Teilhard is probably the non-theologian of the twentieth century with the greatest impact on what theology is doing. Teilhard spoke to the modern world with radiant faith, and his achievement let others see that a radically new type of theology was possible. Theology moved from an essentialist outlook and terminology to speak of present concerns in a contemporary idiom." And Thomas Merton said of one page of *The Divine Milieu,* where "the Christian is not asked to swoon in the shadow, but to climb in the light, of the Cross," that "no finer and more contemplative page has been written in our century." Meanwhile, novelists like Graham Greene and Flannery O'Connor have felt his influence, as have political leaders like Sargent Shriver, who quoted him at the Democratic convention in 1972, and Mario Cuomo, who said Teilhard first convinced him that "God did not intend this world only as a test of our purity, but rather as an expression of his love; that we are meant to live actively, totally, in this world and in so doing make it better for all whom we can touch."

That is the message of *The Divine Milieu,* a short series of reflections, prayers and notes, written for "the waverers," those who feel that God and the world are pulling them in opposite directions. His goal is to provide nourishment for the love of God and a healthy love of the world, teaching his readers to not merely make an act of the will to "purify" one's intentions, but to collaborate in God's work of continuing creation. In short, Teilhard's vision overcomes the general notion that time spent in the office, studio, fields or factory is "time diverted from prayer and adoration."

Teilhard died in New York City on Easter Sunday 1955. That year I graduated from Fordham; then, after two years in the anti-aircraft artillery in Germany, I entered the novitiate at St. An-drew-on-Hudson. There, as part of our daily labor, I cut the grass in the graveyard, clipping around the base of a plain, gray stone marked, incompletely, "Teilhard," never guessing that beneath the sod this great mystic who had studied the earth so intimately and who had so spiritualized matter in his philosophy, was now mingled with the clay from which we all had sprung. Within a few years we would be reading his works, just translated into English—though his theology was considered suspect—because in their openness and optimism they caught the spirit imagination of our generation and freed us from the rigid formulas of thesis scholasticism.

During our theological training we called on him in the now-forgotten controversy over the so-called "hyphenated" priest: the hypothetical identity crisis brought on when priests, caught up in rebuilding the secular city, also became factory workers, lawyers, doctors, congressmen, clowns, and artists as well as preachers and professors. Somehow, the debate died. Perhaps those who couldn't take the tension left. Others printed Teilhard's prayer on their ordination cards: "To the full extent of my power, *because I am a priest,* I wish from now on to be the first to become conscious of all that the world loves, pursues and suffers . . . to become more widely human and more nobly of the earth than any of the world's servants . . ."

33

Death, An Act of Communion

KARL RAHNER, S.J., *The Love of Jesus and the Love of Neighbor* (1983)

To consider Karl Rahner, S.J., the great German theologian who died at the age of eighty in 1984, as an "author" from whose books we select one representative work that would nourish our belief would both fail to do him justice and miss the main point of his life and his impact on religious thought.

A scholar, a transcendental Thomist theologian who incorporates the insights of existentialism, a teacher and spiritual mentor, a courageous independent thinker who continually applies his theological method to contemporary moral and pastoral problems, a loyal servant of the Church, who suffered Rome's censures in the late 1950's, who loved the Church enough to call attention to its failings, Rahner—whose collected essays and talks and multi-volumed *Theological Investigations* total over four thousand books and articles to his name—was the greatest intellectual force within the Church in the twentieth century.

He was also a holy and humble man who said that the best way to learn to pray is to fall on one's knees.

There are excellent collections of passages from Rahner's works, like *The Practice of Faith*, a compilation of his thoughts on the spiritual life; and *A Rahner Reader*, edited by the philosopher, Gerald McCool, S.J. But his fundamental work is *Foundations of Christian Faith: An Introduction to the Idea of Christianity* (1976). This is, to an extent, a summing up of his life's work as a philosopher and theologian. And for someone who wants to compare two giants in their summations, it should be compared with Hans Küng's *On Being a Christian,* which reached out to both the educated priests (Hans Küng told me that he thought the greatest impact of his book might have been on fellow priests) and to marginal believers at a time when educated people were yearning most anxiously to have Jesus Christ explained to them in a frank and intelligent way.

Rahner addresses himself "to readers who are educated to some extent and who are not afraid to 'wrestle with an idea,' " and he hopes that he will "find readers for whom the book is neither too advanced nor too primitive." Anyway, it's a rewarding workout—perhaps best read systematically in a discussion group or slowly over several months.

How can I, who am not a professional theologian, share my limited but deeply-felt experience with this pivotal thinker with readers like myself—men and women anxious either for some new light on an old truth or for some theological organizing principle that will bring order to disparate thoughts? Perhaps by listing three of the many areas where, for men and women of my generation, Rahner's ideas have had the greatest impact.

(1) *The Anonymous Christian.* A "theological anthropology" in which we, through an analysis of our own experience, of our openness to ultimate reality, to God, free ourselves from the long-time artificial distinction between nature and grace, between the so-called natural and supernatural realms of existence. Rather, as Father Richard McBrien expresses it in *Catholicism,* "God is not 'a' Being separate from the human person. God is Being itself, permeating the person but transcending the person as well. Because God permeates as well as transcends us, there is no standpoint from which we can 'look at' God objectively, in a detached manner, as it were. God is always present within us, even before we begin the process, however tentatively and hesitantly, of trying to come to terms with God's reality and our knowledge of God."

This understanding of how God is present to all persons leads to Rahner's extremely influential, and controversial, idea of the "anonymous Christian," wherein even an atheist could be con-

sidered a Christian, because everyone's experience of the tran-
scendent, of "absolute mystery," is an experience of God: "The
person who accepts a moral demand from his conscience as *absolutely* valid for him and embraces it as such in a free act of af-
firmation—no matter how unreflected—asserts the absolute
being of God, whether he knows or conceptualizes it or not, as
the very reason why there can be such a thing as an *absolute moral
demand at all*" (*Theological Investigations,* IX,9).

Of course this idea that one's "Christian" commitment may
be "anonymous," namely Christian without being "religious" in
the traditional sense, was revolutionary in the impetus it gave to
"secular Christianity," the pursuit of religious goals in the secular
world and on secular terms.

(2) *Christ Our Brother.* Writing in *Commonweal,* theologian
Robert Imbelli calls *The Love of Jesus and the Love of Neighbor* "one
of Karl Rahner's last gifts to his fellow believers, the mature sim-
plification of a life's journey." It is here where Rahner—echoing
his idea that sometimes the best way to discover what prayer is
is to fall on one's knees—says: "You are only really dealing with
Jesus when you throw your arms around Him and realize right
down to the bottom of your being that this is something that you
can still do today." As Imbrelli explains, "It is not the idea of
Jesus, nor the memory of Jesus, nor the cause of Jesus which
saves. It is the person who loved and was crucified and is risen
who is the Savior of the world."

Although at first glance it may seem that there are few men
more distant from one another than Rahner and Thoreau, both
build their systems on the same principle which is at the center
of American spirituality: the close, sometimes ruthless, analysis
of personal experience. As Rahner says, we cannot understand
words like *love* and *fidelity* on first hearing; we can do so only by
"gathering together our life experiences while listening to
them—slowly, patiently, ever and again listening to our own
lives—just as someone might collect fresh spring water in a
beaker as it wells up slowly out of the earth."

This analysis leads us to see how we, as human beings, necessarily commit ourselves to others, how we can love a person

who is far away, how love can triumph over time and space, how we read Scripture in the way two lovers gaze at one another, and how Jesus, by the power of the Holy Spirit, presents himself for our embrace as our model and our friend.

Rather than his divinity making Jesus appear more remote from us, in Rahner's theology Jesus' divinity is his Messiahship: " 'Messiah' means the vehicle and bearer of a definitive message that can basically no longer be transcended, a message in which God definitively 'commits himself.' " Thus, in Jesus, God comes absolutely close to us, and invites us to love one another with the same love he has given us. Rahner shows how love of neighbor is an antecedent condition for love of God, and how there is no love for God that is not, in itself, already a love for neighbor. In short: "God is not in competition with human beings."

Then, in a marvelous, pastoral, practical coda that swells up from his theology, he spells out some of the ethical consequences of sharing this love in the modern world. He shows how Christian communion generates a political responsibility, rejoices that modern means of communication have increased our opportunities for more intense forms of human nearness, welcomes the gradual breaking down of nineteenth century religious individualism, and respectfully slaps the wrists of ecclesiastical power people who have abused their authority in the defense of orthodoxy: "Could a Teilhard de Chardin really not have been dealt with in a more brotherly fashion in Rome?"

(3) *Preparing for Death.* The famous Chicago activist of the 1960's, Saul Alinsky, the community organizer who knew how to get poor neighborhoods to unite against oppressive power structures, often told his followers that he attained true freedom when he accepted the fact that he was going to die.

At that moment he knew that none of his enemies could frighten him. Alinsky was a Marxist-Jewish-agnostic who loved to work with poor Catholic parishes. His friend Jacques Maritain described Alinsky as a saint. In some ways he sums up Rahner's idea of the anonymous Christian and his notion of death as the final expression of who we are. Knowing that we are to die intrinsically determines the whole of life; and, in mortal anguish, the fundamental decision that we have made throughout the pattern of our whole life about our relationship to God determines the character of our final moment. We are at the end what we have always been.

Leo O'Donovan, S.J., perhaps Rahner's outstanding interpreter, writes in *Theological Studies:* "As Rahner himself approached death, he seemed to see the cross ever more clearly focusing the solidarity of Christ with men and women throughout history and with the God who in history offers life to them all." Leo's observation reminded me of the dying words of Prince Andre in Tolstoy's *War and Peace,* "It's all so simple."

When Rahner's mother died in 1976 at the age of 101, friends found a handwritten page in her missal quoting the prayer of Teilhard de Chardin, "It is not enough that I should die while communicating. Teach me to treat my death as an act of communion."

Prolific as he was, always willing to keep talking about his constantly growing spiritual understanding, Rahner composed his own final prayer several times. One of the best is in a talk he gave in Freiberg, his birthplace, in 1984: "I can only, stammering, point out how one can in anticipation await 'The One who is to come' by experiencing the descent of death itself as the very ascent of what is coming. Eighty years is a long time. However, for each one the life span allotted to him is but a brief moment in which what should be becomes."